CHINESE TEXTILES

CHINESE TEXTILES

VICTORIA & ALBERT MUSEUM · FAR EASTERN SERIES

VERITY WILSON

V&A PUBLICATIONS

First published by V&A Publications, 2005
V&A Publications
160 Brompton Road
London SW3 1HW

Distributed in North America by Harry N. Abrams, Inc., New York

ISBN 1 85177 438 6

Library of Congress Control Number 2005923380

Designed by Nigel Soper
New V&A photography by Sara Hodges of the V&A Photographic Studio

Front jacket illustration: embroidered satin bag with European lace
    trimming (see plate 9)
Back jacket illustration: silk dress lengths (see plate 90)
Frontispiece: embroidered and couched silk hanging (see plate 78)

Printed in China

V&A Publications
160 Brompton Road
London SW3 1HW
www.vam.ac.uk

Acknowledgements

This book benefited
greatly from the writings
and opinions of many
scholars and students.
They showed me different
ways of looking at the
Chinese textiles in the
Victoria and Albert
Museum in London. My
thanks go to those who
invited me to speak about
the textiles at conferences
and seminars while
studying, and puzzling
over, the collection. Craig
Clunas, Dorothy Ko and
Zhang Hongxing
especially convinced me
the subject was worth
pursuing.

CONTENTS

1
SETTING THE SCENE: CHINESE TEXTILES IN LONDON

AT THE END OF THE NINETEENTH century there were 145 Chinese textiles, including items of dress, in the Victoria and Albert Museum (plates 1 and 2). There are now nearly 4,000. This book is a contribution to the ever-growing history of these textiles.

There are several ways in which the collection can be understood. In its early days it was not developed by trained textile scholars, for the study of textiles was hardly considered a discipline at the time. Neither, initially, was it nurtured by experts in the field of Chinese studies. The textiles stand as a testimony to the West's long-standing and sometimes predatory involvement with China, although the museum itself never acquired pieces directly from there until recent times.

The collection is mediated firstly through the intuition and eye of the collectors, dealers and donors who sold or gave items to the museum, and secondly through the personal judgement and knowledge of curators who over the years of the V&A's existence have always sanctioned Chinese textile acquisitions. The museum's long collecting history therefore partly predates the period of honed textile and sinological study. As a result, what may seem to be a rather haphazard collection is actually one full of interest and visual appeal.[1]

What is in the collection? If a chronological view is taken of the V&A's holdings, the dynastic periods of China's history are not evenly represented. There are some very ancient items, which come from Chinese Central Asia. A near-complete canopy from the Buddhist cave temples near the town of Dunhuang (plate 3) is one example from around 600 early pieces. It is given a date between the eighth and tenth centuries AD and was originally suspended over an image. Made from hemp, a durable fabric that has survived the centuries well, it is painted with lotuses in a circular and four-corner arrangement, with flaps designed to imitate a textile altar valance with streamers. Due to the advocacy of two staff members of the Department of Textiles in the 1920s, the museum secured this early testimony of China's pre-eminence in the textile arts on long loan. The fragments of hemp, silk and wool recovered from what we now call the Silk Road region

1 Embroidered silk
wall panel (detail)
Women in a garden setting
c.1800–50
Whole hanging 340.4 x 50.8cm
V&A: 792-1853
This embroidery is the first
Chinese textile to be registered
in the V&A's records. It was
purchased in 1853 for 4 pounds
7 shillings and 6 pence.

2 Four folio plates of Chinese designs, chromolithographs From Owen Jones, *The Grammar of Ornament*, first published in 1856. Owen Jones (1809–74) produced his *Grammar* in order to establish a valid taxonomy of design. Some of the Chinese examples were taken from textiles then in the museum though today it is impossible to match them to surviving pieces.

3 Canopy, hemp cloth
with painted decoration
AD 700–1000
139 x 139 cm
Ch.00381
Stein Loan Collection

4 Fragment of silk damask
1300–1600
19 x 14 cm
V&A: 7052-1860.
Bock Collection

by Sir Marc Aurel Stein (1862–1943) mostly range in date from the first
century BC to the tenth century AD.

Moving forwards in time, the ivory-coloured silk damask shown in plate
4 belongs to a group of textiles with monochrome small-scale patterning
that date from China's Yuan dynasty (1279–1368) and Ming dynasty
(1368–1644). These were acquired by the V&A from European church
treasuries in the nineteenth century. The piece cannot be dated accurately,
although its production falls somewhere between the fourteenth and
sixteenth centuries. This type of design configuration, incorporating a fluid
set of motifs, here pomegranate sprays, superimposed on a geometric grid, is
a hallmark of Chinese silks from this period. In view of its Christian church
provenance, it might have originally been part of a vestment.

The period from 1600 to 1750, which takes in the end of the Ming
dynasty and the first part of the Qing dynasty (1644–1911), is represented
in the V&A by boldly patterned tapestry-weave silks. One of them, a
decorative table frontal, is shown in plate 5. A coiled dragon dominates the
design, and a border along the top depicts a pair of long-tailed phoenixes.

5 Table frontal
Tapestry woven silk
*c.*1600–1750
90 x 87 cm
V&A: FE.37-1972
Given by Sir Harry
and Lady Garner

They confront each other across a sun disk which, although now worn away in parts, is woven in gold-wrapped yarn, as is the entire background of the larger section. In addition to this, peacock feather-embellished yarns are interwoven into the scales, feet and face of the dragon, giving the piece an iridescent quality. Many kinds of silk were produced in China during the late Ming and early Qing periods, although this particular type outnumbers others in the V&A's collection.

For the most part, the Chinese textiles in the museum come from the latter part of the Qing dynasty or later, and many of them are illustrated and discussed throughout this volume. The types of textile represented in the collection, of whatever date, can broadly be defined as either clothing or furnishing. Although this book will not deal at length with the fashioning of the self through dress, there is information about material used for clothing of different kinds (plate 6). As well as dress lengths, the museum's collection includes examples of religious pictures, chair and cushion covers, table and wall decorations, carpets and celebratory hangings. There are also some pictorial pieces in the form of textile scrolls and albums.

The V&A has not, however, embraced several kinds of Chinese textile that are well represented elsewhere. From the chronological survey above, it is apparent that the museum did not choose to augment its collection with precious material from the seventh to the fifteenth centuries that became available in the closing decades of the twentieth century.[2] Another area of collecting activity pursued by other institutions centres around the textile traditions of people who live within China's borders, but who have cultural ties outside China. Historically, this material has been viewed as ethnographic and perhaps beyond the museum's scope. However, reflecting the essentially arbitrary nature of such categorizing systems as 'ethnography' and 'the

6 Length of blue velvet for a woman's robe
Peonies, chrysanthemums and butterflies
1850–80
90 x 75 cm
V&A: 435-1882
This velvet appeared in Stephen Bushell's 1904–6, two-volume seminal work, *Chinese Art*. This was the first book, as opposed to catalogue, to be based on the holdings of a single museum, the V&A. Its textile chapter provides us with the key for the way in which future interpretations of Chinese textiles in the museum were constructed.

7 Embroidered silk
roundel (detail)
Shouxing, God of Longevity
*c.*1860
D.31.5 cm
V&A: 254-1866

decorative arts', the V&A does house a few examples from these officially designated
'national minorities' (V&A T.27 to T.34-1921, FE.97-1983).

A large amount of the V&A's material is worked with embroidery (plate 7). The
collection also includes examples of pattern weaving, velvets and gauzes, as well as
painting and decorative dyeing. Within these categories of use and technique there are
rural fabrics, propaganda images from the Maoist years (1949–76) and, reflecting China's
vast commercial interests from an early era, textiles manufactured there for export to the
West. This last group is discussed in the next chapter, while further chapters deal with
textiles used in interiors, for special occasions and for clothing. These categories are fluid,
however, and pieces that appear in one section might well be candidates for another. The
two closing chapters are concerned with production and acquisition.

The V&A's Chinese textiles are sometimes rather difficult to understand because
many of them defy categorization by the standard practices of the museum, the collector
and the art market. Before moving on to the themed chapters, therefore, a selection of
items is presented to provide an introduction to the range of pieces in the collection.

A brilliant yellow cover is bordered and patterned with kinetic waving lines that seem
to shift across the satin ground (plate 8). Although the hemlines of Qing dynasty dragon
robes are decorated with similar stripes, representing water, their configuration on this
piece does not easily accord with their placement on such a garment. It must have been
embroidered in a studio that regularly carried out work in this patterning, however, for it
was made with a sure hand and is indistinguishable from the type of embroidery that
does adorn the robes.

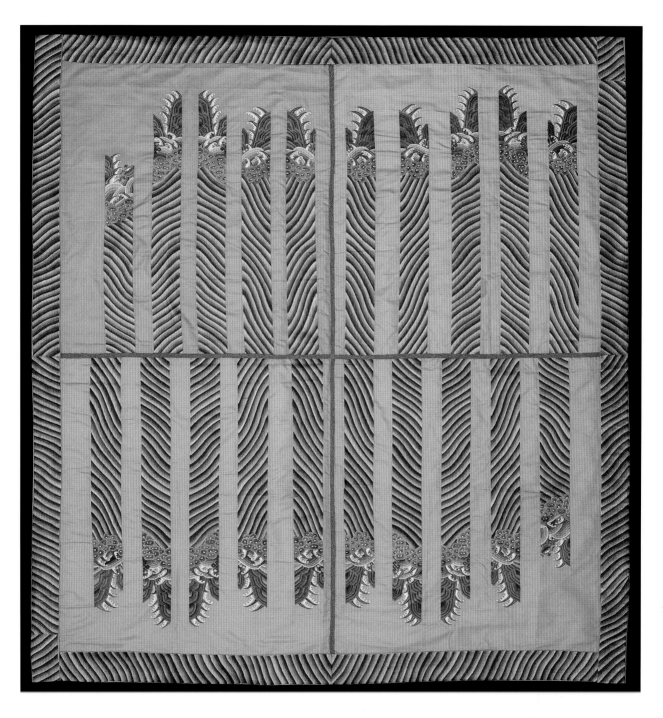

8 Embroidered satin cover
1870–1920
103 x 103 cm
V&A: T.195-1934
Given by T.B. Clarke-Thornhill

9 Embroidered satin bag
with European lace trimming
1700–1800
38 x 33 cm
V&A: 103-1880
Robinson Collection

In the waning years of China's imperial age, at the end of the nineteenth century and beginning of the twentieth century, foreign advisors, soldiers and tourists procured objets d'art specially made for westerners. This might be one of them, its Chinese traditional design superimposed on a shape that could be utilized in a western interior, giving it great appeal for this market. Craft workshops in China were alive to the possibilities of the market and adapted their practices to suit their customers who, increasingly, were westerners with money to spend. Craftspeople who had worked on commissions for the ruling elite and its dependants now had to change their products to survive.

In addition, Europeans themselves altered pieces over the years to fit new needs. This is true of many textiles now in the V&A. More than any other medium, fabric can be cut up, added to and reworked. It is then hard to recover the original context of manufacture and use. A pocket-like bag with pale green silk ribbon ties and European silver bobbin lace trimming (plate 9) was fashioned from a portion of Chinese embroidery. It came into the museum in 1880 from John Charles Robinson (1824–1913), a famous figure in the collecting history of the museum, who helped manage its move from Marlborough House in Pall Mall to the South Kensington site in 1857. He understood that this piece was Chinese and thought it had been adapted in Spain as a burse, a liturgical accessory for the Christian Church that holds the cloth used to cover the bread and wine during the Mass. Its size and shape confirm this, although the ribbon ties and the way it was made to close are out of keeping with such a use and must be later additions.

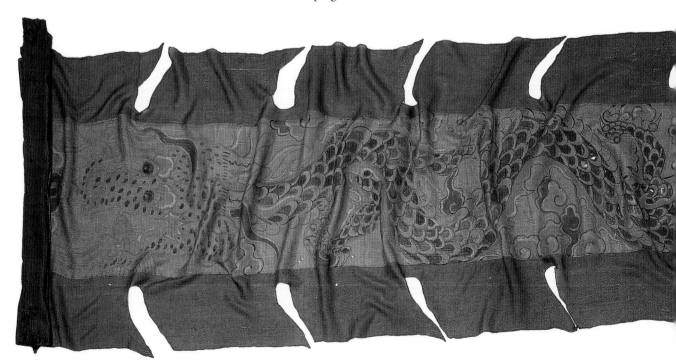

The burse has been given an eighteenth-century date because of the lace, and the Chinese embroidery seems to be from the same century. The design is of a Chinese lantern, the kind that hangs from a hook or pole. It is bedecked with ribbons that float upwards, as if the lantern is being carried aloft. Suspended from the top are pendants dangling from gold dragon finials strung with pearls, flowers and butterflies. Ornamental lanterns are associated with festival times in China and so carry meanings related to happiness. The European seamstress who adapted this Chinese piece was probably unfamiliar with the iconography, but she carefully considered the proportions and incorporated the lantern shape into this small bag with sensitivity. It is a measure of how much fragile textiles are treasured that one piece of silk can have several different lives. The museum is full of such adaptations.

It is perhaps surprising to find among the V&A's Chinese textile collection a set of military banners captured during the Taiping uprising (1851–64) and a programme for a horse-race meeting (plates 10 and 11). Both these pieces, and other items like them, deserve our attention. Each has a story to tell. Although they might sit more comfortably in an army museum, the V&A's set of Chinese banners is a reminder that flags are, by and large, fashioned from textiles, and as such have a place in textile studies. Their design and production are sometimes forgotten facets of textile history, yet flags flutter in the breeze and are rolled and folded and hauled up and down flagpoles because of the supple quality of the fabric used for them.

Thomas Lyster (1840–65), whose descendants donated the flags to the V&A, was a lieutenant with the Royal Engineers and served a term of duty in China as part of the 'Ever-Victorious Army' in 1863. This group of European mercenaries and Chinese regular soldiers were commissioned to repel rebels bent on bringing down the Manchu

10 Military banner, silk with painted decoration
*c.*1863
43 x 426.5 cm
V&A: T.164-1969
Given by Miss C.R. Lyster

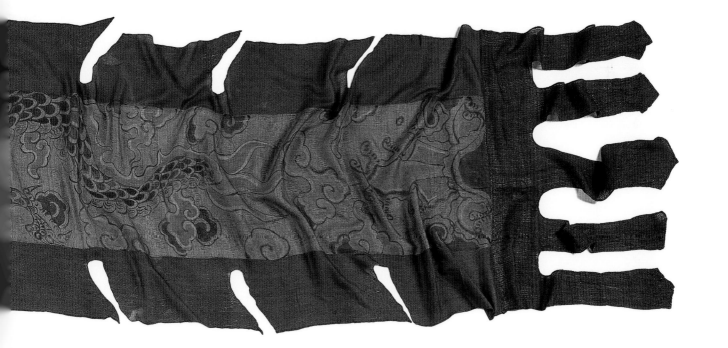

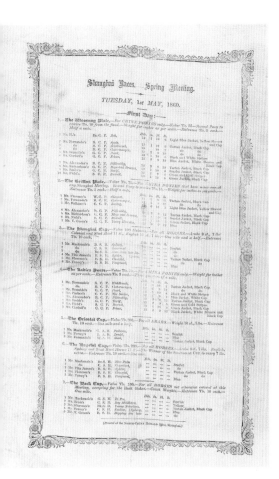

11 Race card, printed satin
dated 1860
34 x 25 cm
V&A: T.163-1935
The Griffins' Plate, listed here as
one of the races, was for ponies
running for the first time.
Young men who joined the East
India Company as novices had
been nicknamed 'griffin'.

imperial family, who ruled as China's last dynasty, the Qing. Despite their eventual defeat, the flowing-haired Taiping ('Heavenly Kingdom') rebels constituted a threatening opposition for over a decade, and their radical ideas attracted Karl Marx (1818–83).[3]

The longest pennant, shown here, unfurls to nearly five metres and is made from thin silk. Its ragged edge is typical of Chinese flags. A dragon is painted along the flag's length, and the sinuous creature would have streamed out from the bamboo pole to which it must have been attached.[4] Lyster, writing to his sister in 1863, tells her he is sending the flag home and says General Charles Gordon (1833–85) gave it to him. This 'rebel trophy', as it was termed by Lyster, was taken at Taicang and its battle-torn condition is a testament to the stout rebel resistance there as recalled by Gordon in his own account of the action.[5]

Another curious textile survival is the printed satin race card (plate 11). It lists the horses and riders for the first day of the Spring Meeting held on 1 May 1860 at the Shanghai racecourse. European-style horseracing began in China in earnest when foreigners were permitted to live and trade in several different cities, termed treaty ports, from 1843. The first racecourse in Shanghai opened in 1851 and by the time of the May 1860 meeting it had twice moved further out to the suburbs. The third racecourse, situated between Tibet Road and Sinze Road, was in operation for only four meetings, this printed programme heralding the inaugural event.

The constant moving of the racecourse further and further out was symptomatic of the inexorable expansion of Shanghai in the late nineteenth and twentieth centuries. During this period, westerners owned and rode their own horses. Part of the lure of living in a place like Shanghai was that pastimes prohibited by their cost back home could be accommodated with relative ease abroad. In the nineteenth century, horses were purchased at a fair price from Mongolian traders, and Chinese grooms who, like other indoor and outdoor staff, were cheap to hire, maintained the animals.

The twice-yearly meetings, held in the autumn as well as the spring, were unmissable events in the social calendar of the well-off, comparatively privileged members of the expatriate community, who lived apart from the Chinese and had their own laws.[6] In August 1860, however, just three months after the events recorded on the satin programme, the Taiping rebels reached the Shanghai racecourse before being overthrown by Gordon. Both the race meeting programme and the Taiping banner, which are contemporaneous, bear witness to the extent of Britain's involvement in China.

The Chinese textile collection in the V&A has a delightful air of eccentricity about it; not all the pieces can be called 'important', although this depends on the definition of such an ambiguous term. 'Important' can often mean very old, or previously owned or connected with someone grand. Some of the Chinese textiles in the collection certainly fall into this category, while others purport to. Connections with the successive Chinese emperors, for example, were one of the signifiers of importance when the collection was being formed. A set of yellow cushion covers and pendants has a good claim to have come from the looting of the Chinese imperial Summer Palace in 1860 (V&A T.134 to

12 Cushion cover
Pattern woven satin
c.1760–1820
73.5 x 71 cm
V&A: T.135-1917
Given by the Dowager
Viscountess Wolseley

13 Embroidered label (detail)
Reverse of another Wolseley
cushion cover
V&A: T.134-1917

T.143-1917). There is contemporary proof of their acquisition by Lt. Col. Wolseley (1833–1913), who procured them at that time and whose family subsequently gave them to the V&A (plate 12).[7] On some of the Wolseley pieces, a carefully embroidered label, sewn onto the reverse before being acquired by the museum, proudly confirms this provenance (plate 13).

The majority of pieces included here have not been illustrated in colour before and some of them have never been on display in the museum. When objects could be safely reinstalled in the V&A galleries after the Second World War (1939–45), Leigh Ashton (1897–1983), a specialist in Chinese art and director of the museum from 1945 to 1955, arranged the collections into Primary Galleries by style, period or nationality, and kept like materials together in Study Galleries. Thus Chinese textiles and dress were displayed in the gallery devoted to Chinese art on the ground floor, as well as upstairs, along with other textiles, in a set of galleries running from north to south of the building. At the beginning of the twenty-first century, they can still be seen, rearranged, in those contexts, as well as in galleries devoted to Chinese export art and British art and design, where they point up the taste for things Asian.[8]

2

CHINESE TEXTILES
AS TRADE GOODS

ALL THE CHINESE TEXTILES now in the Victoria and Albert Museum have of course travelled from Asia to Europe. This chapter focuses on those that were adapted, to a greater or lesser degree, by the Chinese producers to suit the changing needs of foreign markets. The fabrics from China discussed here were all new and known to be so when they were purchased by their original owners. This is another, less-often remarked indicator of export textiles. Only with the increasing presence of westerners within China in the nineteenth century did the search for indigenous antique textiles begin in earnest, and the V&A itself initially only collected contemporary material before it turned its attention to historic pieces in the 1860s. These other kinds of Chinese textiles are discussed in later chapters, although the distinction between the two groups is nearly always blurred, not so much because of how they looked but due to the way in which they were perceived.

The Chinese practised the technique of raising silkworms and extracting silk fibre from them at least 5,000 years ago, as testified by excavated silk fragments. This demanding technology seems not to have been widely developed elsewhere until the third or fourth century AD.[1] The textiles that were woven from the lustrous reeled silk were greatly prized and were exported beyond China's borders. There is early evidence for this in the form of an intact silk saddle blanket found in a tomb in the Altai Mountains of Siberia, dateable to the fifth to fourth century BC.[2]

We have already mentioned in chapter 1 the ancient and medieval textile fragments found in Central Asia, now housed in the V&A, which document the age-old dispersal of Chinese silk. The chain of oases settlements in Central Asia, linked by tracks that later became known as the Silk Road, have played a role in East-West trade and politics since at least the Han dynasty (206 BC–AD 220). Although today this area is Gansu province and the Xinjiang Autonomous Region of the People's Republic of China, it has been a contested region. Its strategic position on the Trans-Asian routes leading out of China to the Indian, Iranian and Graeco-Roman worlds resulted in constant power struggles between local rulers who were bent on making their influences prevail along these vital roads.

It is in this context that the V&A's fragile and fragmentary materials recovered from this area in the first decades of the twentieth century by Sir Marc Aurel Stein (1862–1943) should be viewed. They played a part in the tributary system devised by the Han court and utilized by later Chinese dynasties to pacify people living on China's periphery.

Silk textiles from the professional weaving workshops of China were also used as

19 State bed from
Melville House, Scotland
Crimson Italian velvet,
ivory Chinese silk damask
c.1700
Overall height 462.3 cm
V&A: W.35-1949
Given by the Rt. Hon. The Earl
of Melville

14 Buddhist banner headpiece
Silk with painted decoration
AD 700–1000
42.3 x 85.3 cm
Ch.0086
Stein Loan Collection

devotional donations when one of the world's enduring religions, Buddhism, reached the Silk Road territory from India. From the fourth century AD, this area witnessed a great flowering of Buddhist art, and the Mogao Grottoes at Dunhuang, sometimes known in English as the Caves of the Thousand Buddhas, where many V&A textile fragments originated, was a revered pilgrimage site at the eastern end of the Silk Road. The shifting population of supplicants made offerings there of silk in various forms.

One of the pieces recovered from this remote chapel complex is illustrated here (plate 14). This painted silk, dated to between the eighth and tenth centuries AD, was originally a banner headpiece. It would have formed the upper section of a long, wafting pennant, consisting of several decorated and edged sections, with streamers at either side and at the bottom. A suspension loop was sewn to the point of the headpiece so that the banner could be hung on a pole and carried in procession or left to flutter in a cave chapel. The ivory-coloured silk on which the figure and flowers are painted is itself patterned and this type of monochrome figured textile is one of the great glories of Chinese silk weaving.[3]

While local artisans might have executed the painted and dyed designs on these banners, much of the silk itself was undoubtedly exported from several silk-weaving centres within China. Even when sophisticated silk industries grew up much further west, woven silks from China proper were still famed. They remained desirable commodities, and their designs, as well as the techniques used to pattern them, were ultimately enriched by the eastwards flow of goods, practices and ideas from other great civilizations. The textile fragments now in the V&A, which were found at diverse sites along the Silk Road to the north-west of China's heartland, exhibit an amalgam of iconographic and technological features that continue to present a challenge to their precise identification.[4]

Silks collected from Christian church treasuries and believed to have been in Europe since the time of their manufacture between the late thirteenth century and the sixteenth century provide us with other early examples of the Chinese silk weavers' art (plates 15 and 16). Central Asia, rather than China proper, has been a suggested place of manufacture. Both pieces illustrated here are thought to date from the period when the Mongols ruled China as the Yuan dynasty (1279–1368), as well as controlling a great part of Asia. It has been suggested that entire colonies of weavers were moved westwards from China and eastwards from the Iranian world to Central Asia by the Mongols at this time, and that this might account for the hybrid nature of some of the surviving silks. The evidence is very much stronger for the latter migration of skilled personnel than it is for the former.[5] However, it must be borne in mind that these events are chronicled in Chinese dynastic histories, the sole purpose of which was to put China at the centre of the world, not to record facts. The gathering in of craftsmen from beyond the empire was therefore a narrative to be manipulated in accordance with the aims of the Chinese recording enterprise.

Whatever their true origins, these desirable additions to the European decorative textile repertoire were prized and reverently used as vestments and wrappings for holy relics. This overtly Christian context, however, is enmeshed in another, more worldly, one. These small-scale patterned silks, which seem not to survive in China or Central Asia, are associated with several European Renaissance potentates for whom they were status symbols, fashioned into robes and depicted in paintings of the time. It may have been only subsequently, and with the association of a devout king in mind, that yardage from their clothes was preserved in ecclesiastical treasure rooms.[6]

Very little is known about the past history of these fragments before they entered the museum, and it is the same for a group of silk textiles in the collection, broadly dated between the late thirteenth century and the mid-fifteenth century, that supposedly came from the medieval urban centre of Fustat, which today is in the suburbs of the Egyptian capital Cairo. Two are illustrated here (plates 17 and 18). Today, both are a pale blue and silvery beige. The staining may be due to their having been buried, although no archaeological report exists for them. One appears to be a section of a tunic showing an armhole and a trimmed neck. If this conjecture is correct then it seems likely that the pattern has been misunderstood by the tailor, who may have utilized the fabric 'upside-down'. This is borne out by the incorrect orientation of the circular medallion bearing the stylized Chinese character *shou*, meaning 'longevity', and by the motif of a flaming jewel that fills the spaces in between these medallions. The other fragment illustrated, from the same or similar material, is shown in the 'correct' orientation. This suggests that at least the tailoring was done in a context where the reading of the Chinese character was irrelevant. The weaving may thus have been carried out in China and the silks then exported westwards, or it could have been done outside China by Islamic craftsmen familiar with Chinese patterning. Either scenario is possible, for textiles and other artefacts from several different parts of the world have come from Fustat, an important trading city from the seventh century to the fourteenth century AD, and after that time a refuse site.

Similar textiles have not been found in China and it is possible that these silks were made specially for the Mamluk empire (1250–1517), whose jurisdiction spread across

15 Fragment of silk damask
Palmettes and clouds
1280–1360
16.5 x 10.8 cm
V&A: 7046-1860
Bock Collection

16 Fragment of bi-coloured
silk damask, leaf pattern
1280–1360
17.5 x 15.2 cm
V&A: 7082-1860
Bock Collection

17 Fragment of silk damask
Found in Egypt
1300–1440
53 x 30.5 cm
V&A: 754-1898

18 Fragment of silk damask
Found in Egypt
1300–1440
40.5 x 30 cm
V&A: 1108-1900

Egypt, the Levant and Syria, as well as parts of Libya and Sudan. From surviving Mamluk textiles, it seems that blue was a favoured colour. Mamluk and other textiles from the Islamic world are known to incorporate scripts into their designs, so the inclusion of a longevity ideograph may have been a deliberate move.[7] Although the silks' owners may not have recognized the character or the cloud-like scrolls for what they were, together they gave a very definite Chinese flavour to the material, one that set it apart and therefore rendered it covetable.

How accurately can we date these longevity silks? This particular Chinese character was to be used extensively on different kinds of objects from the Ming dynasty (1368–1644). There is not much evidence for its widespread use before this time, although the relative paucity of early surviving textiles should caution against making generalizations. On the economic front, by 1440 and probably before, there began what was to be a near total, albeit temporary, collapse of cross-cultural trade in luxury goods due to climate change.[8] This overland trade did not revive massively before Portuguese mariners open up the sea routes from 1514, so the silks might be placed somewhere between 1300 and 1440. Their technical features seem to rule out an earlier date, although a later date, after the resumption of international trade, is still possible.

Chinese craft workers were well versed in adapting their products for foreign consumers. Inter-Asian trade was long established before the Portuguese and Spanish entered the market in the sixteenth and seventeenth centuries, followed by other Europeans and then the Americans. These countries' seasonal competitive trading ventures to Asia had broad political and economic consequences, and historians continue to speculate on the outcomes of this international networking. The extant objects from these commercial undertakings are silent witnesses to this interaction. Several examples, as arresting now as they surely were when they were new around 1700, enable us to get a sense of the kinds of textiles shipped from China. Like many export items, none of them throws much light on the Chinese end of the process but the first, the silk on the Melville Bed, provides an unusually rich picture of the context in which it was consumed.

The state bed (plate 19) is a wonderfully preserved piece of furniture from late seventeenth-century Scotland. It epitomizes the indivisible link between the history of Britain and the histories of its overseas engagements, for the elements that make up the whole originated from several sources. One of these sources, the silk-weaving mills of the Lower Yangtze valley in central south China, provided bolts of sheeny ivory silk for use as a lining for the crimson velvet curtains that enclose the bed, as well as for the tester, the headboard and the divided drapery above, the bolster and the fitted counterpane.

The contrast between the dense Genoa velvet and the glossy silk from China is the key to the bed's theatricality. The Chinese satin damask, characterized by its monochrome patterning, catches the light at different angles. In fact, there are two different damasks on the canopied bed. One has a meandering design of flowers and foliage, while the other has a larger, more stylized floral pattern. This last silk, used on the tester and parts of the valance, may represent an adaptation to European taste, whereas the scrolling yardage is typical of that used within China. At the cusp of the century, therefore, these two damasks exemplify the different parameters of the export trade. China was able to satisfy foreign customers with a range of designs, both adapted and indigenous.

19 State bed from Melville
House, Scotland
Crimson Italian velvet,
ivory Chinese silk damask
*c.*1700
Overall height 462.3 cm
V&A: W.35-1949
Given by the Rt. Hon.
The Earl of Melville

The Melville damasks provide a ground for the coronets and initials of the bed's owners, George Melville (*c.*1634–1707) and his wife Catherine. In 1700, this grand item of furniture, together with its textile accessories, formed the showy centrepiece of a specially planned, formal suite of apartments that were made ready in the hope that King William, who ascended the English and Scottish thrones with his wife Mary in 1689, would one day visit Scotland and lodge at Melville House. In one way the Chinese bed silks are a small footnote in the history of British design, but in another they are central to how the riches of empire were amassed from lands beyond the British Isles. Such an expanse of silk from China is a rare survival.[9]

Another, much smaller rarity is the pair of dolls known as Lord and Lady Clapham (plate 20). They are similar in date to the Melville Bed and, although lacking the dramatic quality of the latter, they speak of opulence, the accurate detailing of their sets of removable clothing and accessories exactly replicating the fashions of the day. Their small garments are made from a variety of different materials, among them silk from China. Lady Clapham's dress and underskirt, known as a mantua and petticoat respectively, as well as the cushion at her feet, are all of imported Chinese cloth (plates 21, 22 and 23). The silk, like that of the Melville Bed, is a satin damask, the textile's allure being its monochrome patterning, with the floral designs revealed as the light falls on its surface. Lord and Lady Clapham's nightgowns are also of Chinese silk. The dolls are so named because of their possible connection with the Cockerell family, who came

20–21 Dolls, Lord and Lady Clapham
London, England
Lady Clapham's Chinese silk damask
mantua
1690–1700
Height of seated dolls 56 cm
V&A: T.846 and T.847-1974
Purchased by public subscription

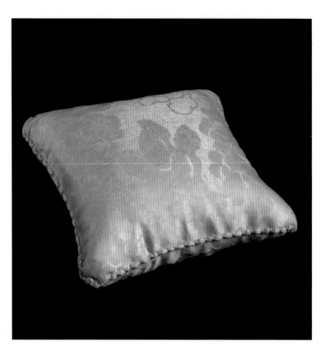

from the Clapham area of south London. They were heirs of the famous journal writer Samuel Pepys (1633–1703), whose diary provides ample evidence for the growing fashion for imported Asian luxuries in late Stuart Britain.[10]

The striped bedcover (plate 24) has also endured intact, although it may not be as early as originally thought when it entered the museum from a London salesroom. It has been variously dated to between the end of the sixteenth century and the eighteenth century. The latter period, or later, now seems most likely. We know that the silver and crimson passementerie and tassels are of European manufacture and come from the nineteenth century or even later. The silk itself exhibits a Europeanized design, similar in formality to one of the Melville damasks, although it is not as well woven. The appealing deployment of stripes, making the colour rather than the patterning the predominant visual force, is not common on Chinese silk for home consumption and there is a similarity between this bedcover and certain northern European, particularly Dutch, silks.

It is still uncertain how exactly western textile designs were transmitted to the workshops of China, and how they were processed once there. The present evidence suggests that written requirements, graphic material in the form of engravings and drawings, as well as actual examples, were among the most likely design sources, at least for ceramics. Bookplates provided the models for European coats-of-arms, favourite subjects for personalized porcelain from China, and these family emblems were also embroidered onto Chinese silk.[11] Chinese textiles for the western export market may have been modelled on actual material, a comparatively easy commodity to ship, but this is still speculative.

The double-headed bird that recurs as a design motif at different periods on Chinese and Central Asian textiles should be mentioned in this context. Originally perhaps an eastern Iranian decorative device, it is seen here at the centre of an embroidered bedcover

22–23 Lady Clapham's petticoat and footrest of Chinese silk damask
1690–1700
V&A: T.846 and T.847-1974
Purchased by public subscription

24 Bedcover
Striped patterned silk
c.1750–1850
European trimming and tassels
c.1850–1920
285 x 203 cm
V&A: FE.5-1977

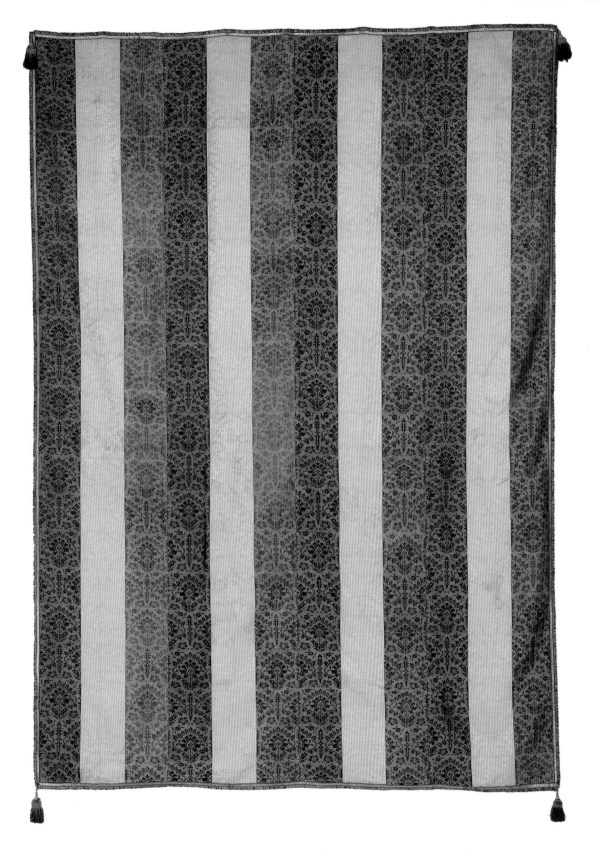

(plate 25). The cover was on display in the museum at some time in the past and a copy of the label exists, dating it to the sixteenth or seventeenth century. The red background silk has faded to a mellow hue and the gold thread, lavishly used all over the cover and particularly on the bird's body and neck, has rubbed and tarnished. Nonetheless, it is possible to imagine how stunning this piece must have been when it was new. The very distinctive way it is embroidered, with lattice gold work and a limited palette of silk embroidery thread in green, blue, yellow and white straight stitches in blocks, has prompted scholars to speculate that such pieces may have been made with a particular clientele in mind, or that they came from a particular group of workshops.[12]

The piece was purchased by the V&A as early as 1855 and, although the bird on it is often called an eagle, it is not especially eagle-like, its long, narrow neck with blue crest feathers being more reminiscent of the pelican of Christian iconography. The double-headed bird, a symbol with many manifestations and allegiances, is also represented in

25 Embroidered silk
bedcover (detail)
1550–1750
Whole cover 259 x 208 cm
V&A: 4016-1855

the V&A's Chinese textile collection by several examples and fragments that have been well used in their past lives (V&A 922-1899, T.215 and T.217-1910).

Although the picture of Saint Sebastian (plate 26) was in Britain by 1921, the year it was acquired by the V&A, it is possible that it was made for a Christian community in Asia rather than in Europe. Pieces like this therefore blur the distinction between 'export' and 'indigenous' art. Difficult to date with any precision, but made during China's Qing dynasty (1644–1911), it came into the museum in poor condition, suggesting prolonged use. The much-faded red background satin is made up of two sections of cloth. The central, vertical seam would have been hidden by the trunk of the tree to which Sebastian is tied, although today the embroidery stitches have completely deteriorated in this area, leaving hundreds of small needle holes. Two other lines, parallel to the long edges and caused by tension, show where the picture has been stretched around a frame. Sebastian's body is very finely worked with close, straight stitches showing the musculature of the saint's torso. The blood oozing from the wounds is painted over the stitching. On either side of the figure, the palm-like trees weighed down with yellow fruit are a reminder of east Asia's climatic diversity. Sebastian is said to have been a Roman soldier persecuted for his Christian faith under the Emperor Diocletian (r.AD 284–305). The arrows that penetrated his body miraculously failed to kill him and he was eventually stoned to death.

The impressive scale of the figure is not so unusual in China, for equally large depictions of Chinese Buddhist and Daoist immortals exist, but the obvious human dimension of the near-naked Sebastian, awkwardly bound to a tree and pierced with arrows, is a western and Catholic Christian manifestation. The rawness of such Catholic images presented a problem when European Jesuits and other missionary orders attempted to import Christianity into China from around 1600. Their Chinese converts were relatively few before the nineteenth century, a fact that may owe something to the iconographic incompatibility of such graphic scenes of mutilation with Chinese canons of taste in visual imagery.

The material culture of Christianity in China did, however, chime in one aspect with Chinese expectations of pictures, including those made from silk. There was a shared stress on pictures relevant to specific occasions, whether Chinese festivals such as the New Year, or the festivals of the Christian liturgical year. The latter, of course, included the feast days of saints, the kind of occasion on which this large hanging of Saint Sebastian, and another like it of Saint Anthony of Padua, also in the V&A's collection (V&A T.246-1921), might plausibly be thought to have been exhibited.[13]

One other possibility that might be explored in connection with this icon of Catholic Christianity is that it was manufactured in the Philippines, a Spanish colony from the middle of the sixteenth century. There, the hybrid culture of indigenous peoples and Chinese immigrants was subjected to the full rigour of Iberian Counter-Reformation ideology, which consequently produced, by persuasion or coercion, a largely Catholic population. The Chinese, who had been settled in the Philippines long before the Spanish arrived on the scene, initially came as traders. The artisans who followed may have been responsible for this kind of Christian embroidered hanging, as well as other types of textile. Several bedcovers in the V&A have provenances that could support this view, although their exact history is not now verifiable. The bedcover detail pictured here

dates from the eighteenth or early nineteenth century (plate 27). It has a Philippines provenance via Portugal and is similar in layout and execution to others in the museum. They each have a central medallion surrounded by floral swags and borders, and an applied, striped fringe. The white or pastel background is a standard feature of such bedcovers. We should not rule out the possibility of there being several centres making almost identical products both in mainland China and in the Philippines. Connections between the two Chinese populations were always strong. In Spanish times there was a frequent exchange of goods, ideas and capital via the flat-bottomed, high-prowed boats we know as junks, between China's southern provinces and the Philippines.

Further evidence for this Chinese diasporic networking is provided by a class of textile, mainly later in date than the bedcovers, whose name in Spanish, *mantón de Manila*, speaks of a connection with the capital city of the Philippines. Embroidered and fringed silk shawls in several colours and designs started to be made for export in the first half of the nineteenth century. In 1821, Seville in southern Spain began to trade directly with Manila, and it is from this time that depictions of Spanish women wearing such shawls abound. It seems that Chinese embroidery workshops in south China or Manila initially produced a specialized product for a dedicated market, which then expanded to include other parts of Europe as well as the Americas.

An example from the V&A's collection of twenty shawls is illustrated here (plate 28). Effectively embroidered in white on a black ground and with a long, swaying fringe, it

26 Embroidered silk picture of St Sebastian
1700–1900
170 x 137.2 cm
V&A: T.245-1921

27 Embroidered silk bedcover (detail)
1750–1850
Whole cover 269 x 226 cm
V&A: 900-1900

28 Embroidered silk shawl
Silk fringe
1880–1920
140 x 148 cm plus 47 cm fringe
V&A: FE.29-1983
Given by Mrs N. Iliffe
From the collection of her
mother, Lady Pickthorn

was worn folded into a large triangle. These shawls were never a part of the Chinese clothing tradition, although they survive in large numbers outside China and their production continues today. In Victorian and Edwardian Britain they were not always part of the fashion mainstream, but became imbued with Bohemian associations both when worn and when draped over furniture as part of an artistic interior decor.[14]

Consumers have always been avid shoppers for goods from abroad. The extent to which a country of origin adapts its products for an overseas market is finely judged, and we should not assume that this was any less of a challenge historically than it is today. With regard to China, the precise nature of the adaptation is difficult to gauge for past periods. Not only are the extant objects from both East and West chance survivors, but also our perception of what is, or is not, Chinese is bound up with our shifting attitudes towards that country.

Apart from the shawls that had their origins in an Hispanic trading nexus, one of the most ubiquitous items made in China for export to the West is the bedcover. Several have already been discussed, and another type, exemplified by the yellow bedcover and details of a white one in plates 29, 30, 31 and 32, perhaps appear to contain more Chinese elements than the others. There are butterflies, long-tailed birds, lions with curly backs, pointed peaches, 'fingered' citrus fruits, blossoming branches and peony sprays, all motifs found on native Chinese artefacts. However, in making the argument for these covers' Chinese character, it would be wrong to suppose that everyone who saw them unambiguously pronounced them to be Chinese, and it is not only Chinese people who fail to recognize so-called 'export art'. The motifs, loosely disposed around a central circle on both covers, are distinctly export orientated.

The painted silks that came out of Canton (the English name for Guangzhou) from the eighteenth century onwards are so similar to the wallpapers also manufactured there for sale to westerners that it seems probable they were executed in the same workshops. Neither wallpaper nor painted silk of this sort played a large part in the Chinese

29 Embroidered silk bedcover
1770–90
218.4 x 179.1 cm
V&A: T.387-1970
Given by Mr and Mrs G.H.G.
Norman

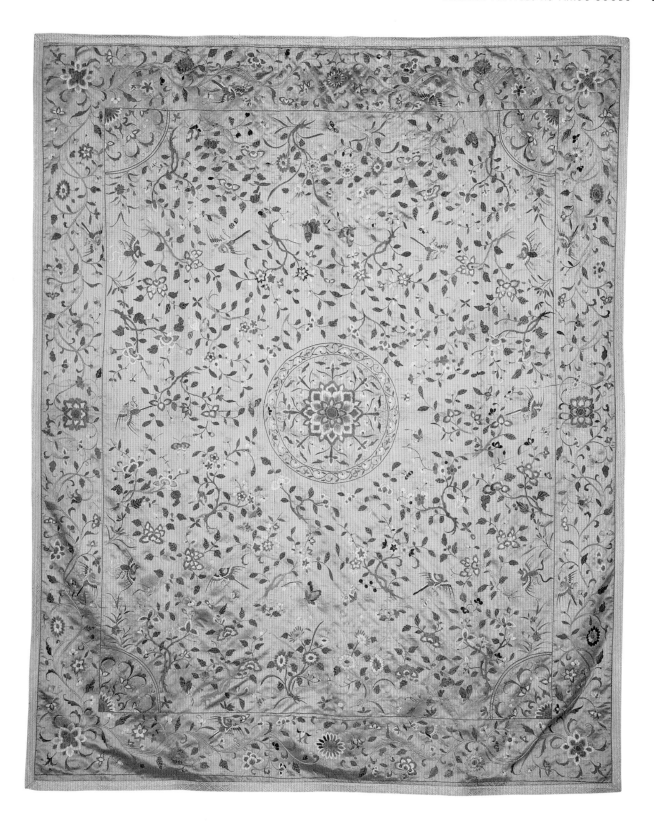

decorative interior, but there had long been a role for anonymous jobbing painters in China who produced batches of near-identical pictures. Surviving painted silk examples in the V&A show that this type of cloth was used in Europe for both clothes and furnishings. The museum's collection includes lengths made up into a dress, dated to between 1760 and 1765, that belonged to Eva Garrick, the wife of the actor David Garrick (V&A T.593-1999), a set of Christian vestments (V&A T.89 to T.93-1923) and a piece used to upholster a European chair (V&A T.179-1965), both also from the eighteenth century, as well as a panel of painted gauze-weave silk sewn and padded to form a cot quilt (V&A T.119-1949) from the early nineteenth century.[15]

It is not known how the appealing eighteenth-century painted silk panel shown here (plate 33) was used. It is unlined and its pictorial composition suggests a wall hanging. The border design around the edges is not necessarily commensurate with face-on viewing, however, so it could be a bedcover. Whatever its purpose, its generally excellent condition may indicate that it was never used much at all. Even so, the painted surface is cracked and rubbed in several places, highlighting the inherent vulnerability of such surface-decorated silks. Charm and cheapness took precedence over durability.

True to the V&A's original guiding mission when it was founded, designers and marketing executives still take inspiration from the museum's collections. They frequently request to see the Chinese textiles and invariably choose to reproduce and

30–32 Embroidered silk bedcover (details)
1720–90
Whole cover 256.5 x 274 cm
V&A: T.93-1949
Given by Mrs Montagu

33 Painted silk bedcover or hanging
1760–1800
274 x 251 cm
V&A: T.3-1948
Given by Mr G.W. Dobson

reinvent these particular painted silks. Their appeal has been long lived, and the tried and tested formula, much used on export art, of a profusion of different seasons' flowers blooming together, is a winning one. Made in China though these silks undoubtedly were, the way they look is not really Chinese at all but a result of the specific market conditions prevailing at the time.

Another very large decorative textile in the collection could have been used as a bedcover or an ornamental throw. A detail is shown here (plate 34). It is far heavier than the painted piece, being made from a dense, cream satin, and having a lining as well as a deep fringe all around the edges. The subject matter is one that occurs in Chinese painting. Birds flocking around a mythical phoenix seems to have been a popular subject from the Ming dynasty. This twentieth-century embroidery represents a revival and reworking of the theme, which does not refer back to any kind of narrative text, although foreigners have sometimes tried to construct a story around the scene. It is possible to identify many of the birds as they fly and strut through a watery, flower-filled landscape that is embroidered with great virtuosity. There is no sense here, as there is in the case of some other export embroideries, that the ground was covered with the minimum effort possible. On the contrary, the coloured silk threads are closely packed together within each motif, and there is a variety of stitching techniques; these required the embroiderer to go back over areas already filled in. The amount and quality of the embroidery involved suggests we should revisit the old adage of 'earlier means better workmanship'. A distinctive ivy-leaf trailing border, not seen in this detail, the pale turquoise tones, the mustard yellows and salmon pinks are all indications of twentieth-century work.

Due to the western re-evaluation of handmade things as a result of high levels of industrialization and mechanization in the West, this skilful hand embroidery may be connected to the demands of a more discerning clientele, coupled with astute Chinese entrepreneurship. Embroidery workshops in China and Chinese-run businesses in other parts of Asia producing this type of work published pattern books from which customers could choose designs and colours (page 101).

Another facet of the export textile trade is exemplified by a curtain, one of a pair, shown here (plate 35). The fabric is ramie, a semi-transparent, linen-like material. Each curtain is embroidered with white twisted thread in a pattern of birds and butterflies among flowers and bamboo, in an arrangement familiar from other export textiles and wallpaper. There is a drawn thread work border around the sides and along the hem. The American donor's family had links to the China trade and it is believed by them (although not definitively known) that four pairs of curtains like this were commissioned from China in the early part of the nineteenth century.

It is not known whether the relatively plain aesthetic of such pieces was the particular preserve of New England households at this time. For a later period, however, from the second half of the nineteenth century and on through the first half of the twentieth century, there are museum examples of white on white or cream on cream tablecloths and napkins (V&A FE.41-1983, FE. 95 and FE.96-1983). Some are silk and some are ramie, and they incorporate drawn thread work. White work and drawn thread work are part of the western tradition of needlecraft, but dragons often decorate this type of table linen, perhaps as a deliberate signifier of its Chinese origin.

34 Embroidered silk cover
(detail)
*c.*1900–1930
241 x 205.5 cm
V&A: T.108-1962
Given by Miss Frances R. Wills

35 Curtain of
embroidered ramie
1830–40
248 x 99 cm
V&A: FE.150-1983
Given by Mrs Perkins H. Bailey
In memory of her husband

With these souvenirs we have clearly moved on from the days of Silk Road caravans travelling overland across the roof of Asia. The subsequent age of East India Company trading, which was dependent upon the winds and ocean tides and conducted solely through the southern Chinese port of Canton, was also over by the mid-nineteenth century. Although in 1780 there were some who thought the British empire would not survive and increase as it did, after 1842 the repercussions of the drug trade in Asia led to greater opportunities for western intervention in China. Although China was never part of Britain's formal empire, foreigners began to live and do business there from the 1860s. Moreover, by 1902 the curiosity that China had aroused in Europe, America and Japan was satisfied by a growing tourist industry.

Far from being put off travelling to China in the aftermath of the Boxer Rebellion (1900), a peasant revolt culminating in a siege of the foreign legations in Beijing, there was a spate of activity, with Bradshaw's, a British travel itinerary firm, adding a 'China Route' supplement to its India handbook in 1903. With Trans-Asian railway networks and steamship lines pushing further east, travel companies were organizing China tours and these were not just for the rich. Many guidebooks were published around this time and most of them included tips on shopping. One of them, Ogden's *Notes on Sightseeing and Shopping in Peking* published for the United States Armed Forces and reprinted several times in the 1930s, ranked shopping with sightseeing as a necessary and pleasurable activity (plate 36).[16]

36 Panel from a shop front
Carved wood
From a silk store in Beijing. Several carved wooden panels of a shop front were donated to the V&A in 1924 by a British diplomat, Mr E.L. Cockell (d.1936). He believed them to date from the Ming dynasty (1368–1644). The characters across the top, loosely translated, give the name of the firm as 'Myriad Brocaded Silk Company'. After being on display before the Second World War, these shop panels were disposed of in the 1950s.

White work and coloured cross-stitch embroideries were favourite purchases, and the section on shopping in *Peking and the Overland Route*, published in Shanghai in 1917 by the early giant of the travel industry Thomas Cook and Son, particularly singles out grass cloth, the common name for ramie, as being a very effective handicraft. Individual tourists in China bought embroideries of several sorts, and they could also be obtained by consumers in Europe, particularly women, who never had the opportunity to travel there but who purchased them in drapery and linen shops, and in department stores.[17]

As mentioned already, like the Indian subcontinent, China had vast textile trading connections within Asia itself and produced goods to suit different regions. The products of these specific textile traditions are not well represented in the V&A's China collection, but woollen hangings like the one pictured here (plate 37) are examples of a class of textiles made in north China for the Japanese market. Some surviving pieces preserved in Japan may date as far back as the sixteenth century, and rewoven copies of these treasured older pieces are still used to decorate festival floats there.[18] Their distinctive designs were repeated through the Japanese Meiji period (1868–1912) and on into the 1920s and possibly later. Some of them found their way to the West. They are described in an English-language Chinese commercial guide from the 1860s.[19]

In our present state of knowledge it is not possible to date the V&A's three examples accurately (V&A T. 158-1966, T.193 and T. 194-1968). The piece illustrated entered the museum via the collecting endeavours of Jaap Langewis, an anthropologist and collector from the Netherlands whose name is associated with the Japanese folk textiles with which he enriched the V&A's holdings. He himself recognized it as being from China, although used

37 Flat-weave rug
*c.*1850–1940
187.9 x 134.5 cm
V&A: T.158-1966
Langewis Collection

in Japan. A letter from the Dutch scholar preserved in the V&A's archives states that the piece is probably mid-eighteenth century in date, and 'is woven of hog bristles on a cotton ground'.[20] It seems more likely to be made from goat hair, the pattern being produced by the tapestry technique. The paired birds are reversed at the top, as if this section was designed to be draped over a bar or piece of furniture and viewed from the opposite side.

3 CHINESE TEXTILES FOR INTERIOR DECORATION

NONE OF THE CHINESE TEXTILES housed in the Victoria and Albert Museum was made to be in a museum. So how were they used in China? This and the next two chapters attempt to answer that question, commencing with a discussion of how such fabrics were used as furnishings in the home.

Although textiles of all kinds were and still are pressed into service for decorating interiors in both China and Europe, the very many Chinese textiles in the V&A that have been altered and remade are symptomatic of a disjunction between the ways textiles were employed in the two cultures. However, there are also textile lengths like those shown in plate 38 that have not been altered in any way and are, in fact, unused. They seem to be furnishing fabrics by virtue of their weight and design, although evidence for how they were used is lacking.

Both lengths are vibrantly coloured in orange, pink and green although their motifs differ considerably. The small repeating design of dragons among clouds comes from a repertoire of traditional Chinese patterning, unlike the carnations against a swirling metallic ground. That the two should occur simultaneously on fabrics at the beginning of the twentieth century is unsurprising, for such terms as 'traditional', 'modern' or 'western', while useful, can never be isolated one from another. The V&A has an abundance of Chinese textiles like these from the late nineteenth and twentieth centuries. The received wisdom that China and its artistic endeavours were in decline during this period has been undergoing thoughtful revision, and pieces such as these dazzling orange bolts help to rectify the misconceptions.

How foreigners view Chinese interiors is coloured by the widely published photographs of the halls of the former imperial palaces, now themselves open as museums.[1] Many cushion covers with yellow grounds thought to be from such palaces survive in western collections, including the V&A collection. Illustrated here (plate 39) is one eighteenth-century example. Nine golden dragons writhe and plunge through coloured clouds bordered by silvery-blue waves. The piece is faultlessly planned and embroidered. The fringe, despite being a good colour match, is a later addition. The museum has some twenty examples of yellow cushion covers. Few are in pristine condition and several have been adapted to a European furnishing aesthetic. Some are embroidered, like the one shown here, some are in silk tapestry weave, while a fewer number are pattern woven (page 16, 17 and 105). All adhere to a design and colour format that at once identifies them as a group even though there are differences in the detailing.

These distinctive covers were undoubtedly preserved because of their connection to the imperial court, and there is no doubt that at least some of them adorned royal

quarters. In this respect they are like the yellow dragon and court robes that are equally sought after and that share some of the same iconography. Frequently occurring main motifs on them are dragons, peaches, longevity characters and bats.

Chinese cushion covers were packed tight with wadding. Rectangular ones were used for seats, often fitting into specially designed depressions, while shaped ones stood upright against chair backs. Small cushions for supporting the elbows and lower arms were used in conjunction with these two types, being placed on either side of the sitter. The museum has several of these, all in their original padded state (V&A T.202-1926, T.749-1950 and T.123-1966), and an embroidered pair is shown here (plate 40). These date from the late eighteenth or nineteenth century and are fashioned from panels to form a sphere. The original sewing lines are worked in carefully spaced yellow silk running stitch and the embroidery, in shades of red and blue, is matched across the seams. These elbow cushions are undoubtedly a pair, but while large numbers of yellow furnishings survive in many collections, rather few of them seem to be preserved in sets, apart from pairs of elbow rests like these. This has more to do with the piecemeal way

39 Embroidered silk cushion cover
1750–1800
European fringe, *c.*1900
83 x 104 cm
V&A: T.240-1959
From the estate of Her Late Majesty Queen Mary (1867–1953)

40 Pair of embroidered silk
elbow cushions
1780–1850
23 cm
V&A: FE.138-1983
Addis Bequest

such coveted items were released or robbed from the palace precincts during the
nineteenth and early twentieth centuries than with anything pertaining to Chinese
decorating sensitivities.

These types of yellow cushion are perhaps unique to their particular setting. While
pictures of imperial residences might give us an idea of how they were used, it cannot be
assumed that cushions were similarly deployed in more modest family mansions. Rather
few interior views of the latter survive, although literary descriptions and illustrations to
these works of fiction help us understand the layouts of rooms and the disposition of
different textiles within them.

A practice common to many households, including the imperial household, was that
of covering the sides of a table with an ornamental silk cloth. Plate 41 shows a hardwood
table decorated this way. Such textiles have a wide constituency. They were used in
temple spaces and hence are often called 'altar frontals' and, although they may also have
decorated the offering tables of family altars in the home, in late imperial times they were
frequently used in the reception rooms of Chinese mansions, as well as in the town and
city offices of government functionaries. Their distinguishing
features are a rectangular section of decorated cloth and a pelmet
attached across the top edge with, above it, a strong strip of plain
material, often cotton, with loops at either end. The loops are
threaded with tape that then secures the frontal to the legs or around
the top of the table. Sometimes the piece is designed to hang nearly
all around the table. Sometimes it just hangs down the front. Either
way, these textiles are not made to cover the top of a table.

Frontal designs, which can be embroidered or pattern woven,
tend to have a balanced feel about them without being strictly
symmetrical. This is the case with another V&A frontal from the
turn of the twentieth century (plate 42). The pelmet here is straight,
although others are pleated or gathered, and the motifs are worked

41 Embroidered silk table
frontal *c.*1670–1750
79.3 x 262.9 cm
V&A: FE.37-1911
Huali wood table 1550–1650
87.7 x 58.8 cm
V&A: FE.21-1980

42 Embroidered silk
table frontal
1880–1910
91 x 91 cm
V&A: T.264-1929

on a smaller scale than those on the main section. The frontal is unified by the
coordinated colour scheme of blues and white. Antique vases bearing flowers and fruit
encode wishes for luck and happiness.

Cloth skirts for tables can clearly be observed in scroll and wall paintings from the
Buddhist site near Dunhuang in northwest China dating to the tenth century AD. Textile
chair covers, however, our next consideration, appeared a century or so later when the
Chinese relinquished sitting on the floor in favour of sitting on chairs.[2] Little survives in the
way of actual pieces of either furniture or furnishings from these early periods and most of
the V&A's frontals and covers date to the Qing dynasty (1644–1911) or later. The dark
blue satin chair cover pictured here (plate 43), dateable to the eighteenth century, is part of
a set that includes several matching embroidered covers, frontals and pictures. Today, they
have raw edges and are unlined, although this does not prevent an understanding of how
the four compositionally distinct sections of the cover would be arranged on a chair.

The top part drapes over the back rail, thus 'righting' the golden longevity character
shou, which here appears upside down. The portion showing precious vessels covers the

43 Embroidered silk
chair cover
1750–1820
185.4 x 55.9 cm
V&A: T.177-1948
Vuilleumier Collection,
purchased with a grant from the
National Art Collections Fund

44 Print from *Dianshizhai
Pictorial*, June 1885
This illustration, by Wu Youru,
depicts the signing of the peace
treaty after the Sino-French
War (1883–5). The delegates sit
on chairs with decorative covers,
the high command is behind a
table with a frontal around the
legs and the walls are hung with
scroll-like floral panels.

inside back of the chair, and the ogival central panel, outlined in gold and filled with peonies in soft greens and pinks, rests on the seat. The bottom part, with the mythical hoofed and scaled beast, called a *qilin* in Chinese, falls down the front to the floor.

Such covers were used on wooden chairs with or without arms. Unlike the wider and lower couches or throne-like items of furniture of the imperial family or the very wealthy, these did not always support padded cushions. There is some evidence to suggest that these covers sometimes had ties to attach them to the chair. This would offset their tendency to ruckle and slip when someone's weight bore down on them. It is probable that such furnishings were never in fact sat on, although illustrations of interiors from periodicals of the late nineteenth century onwards tell us otherwise. They were probably laid out according to a seasonal schedule or when guests were expected (plate 44).

The preparation of beds in a Chinese household involved textiles of all sorts. Many beds were massive, calling for curtains, valances, pelmets, quilts and pillows to keep out drafts and insects, and to provide comfort and visual appeal. Whether they were framed and canopied beds made of wood, or the raised platform beds of north China made of bricks and heated from beneath (*kang*), they were often used during the daytime as sitting areas, as well as for sleeping at night.[3] Draped bed curtains, which could be held back with decorative metal, wooden or padded textile hooks, were made from silk gauze like the unused lengths pictured here (plate 45). A light and airy fabric, gauze was suitable for Chinese traditional summer clothing and furnishings alike. All these silks have a small paper shop label stuck on one corner confirming that they were bought in

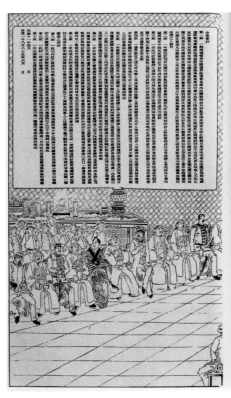

45 Silk gauze lengths
1880–1930
from left to right:
blue with 'endless knots'
V&A: FE.114-1983
345 x 74.7 cm
white with blossoms
V&A: FE.99-1983
568 x 76 cm
red with bats, longevity
characters and 'endless knots'
V&A: FE. 113-1983
356 x 70 cm
bright blue with
geometric pattern
V&A: FE.115-1983
372 x 73.5 cm
Addis Bequest

Beijing under the auspices of the state after 1949, although the textiles themselves date to earlier in the twentieth century or a little before. These ready-printed labels, with information added by hand, give a brief description of the product.

The silk panel illustrated in plate 46 also has such a label, and it tells us that it was woven as a quilt cover. Chinese beds sometimes have two or three quilts neatly folded and stacked up at one end during the day. On this piece, which would have been the top part of the quilt cover, the blue satin ground is brocaded in gold and several colours with traditional iconography. The patterning is arranged in three sections, as is often the case with these covers, with wide bands of repeating designs across the top and a narrower one along the base. The central section is taken up with five four-toed dragons surrounded by Daoist and Buddhist emblems. When made up, some covers have an additional applied broad border in plain-coloured silk all around the edge, and this can extend underneath to form the reverse side.[4]

All the furnishings discussed thus far confirm the widespread use of silk in China. Although silk is seen as a luxurious and prestigious fabric, more people than we might suppose were able to afford it. It was produced within China itself, in many provinces across the country and, over the centuries, a variety of business practices ensured a good supply of various grades of silk. Cotton was extensively used as well, coming into general use in the Ming dynasty (1368–1644), although unlike in the silk industry most producers were farm households up until the end of the nineteenth century. Then, with the introduction of power spinning and, in the twentieth century, mechanized weaving, factory yarn and cloth production greatly increased cotton output. These technical developments were paralleled by equally momentous social changes, which saw the factories in Shanghai absorb great numbers of young female employees. The factories were the crucible for the creation of an urban-based female working class, which had far-reaching implications for China's social and political development as the twentieth century progressed.[5]

Handmade cotton was more durable, but machine-made cotton was cheaper and smoother. In the Maoist years (1949–76) attempts at further improvements were pursued with some vigour but, despite the rhetoric of success, the periodic political crises often meant a decline in standards.[6] The printed cotton lengths for quilt covers (plate 47)

46 Cover for a quilt
Pattern woven silk
1800–1930
234 x 209 cm
V&A: FE.134-1983
Addis Bequest

were purchased in 1978, two years after the death of Chairman Mao. That year saw the beginnings of the Democracy Movement as well as a cautious opening up to foreign commerce with, for example, agreement for a Coca-Cola bottling plant in Shanghai. The general style and quality of these lengths is representative of the top end of production under Mao. During his regime cotton rationing and poor distribution networks severely limited people's access to such goods, although propaganda photographs went some way towards concealing these deficiencies (plate 48). By the time the V&A's lengths were made, in around 1978, observers were noticing the increased prevalence of printed designs on cotton and silk.[7]

Both lengths are decorated with peacocks and large flowers. This patterning adheres to the design fundamentals of the 1950s, which were to be expounded again in 1979 in a book published in Shanghai for students and practitioners.[8] Interspersed among the birds and flowers are vignettes in paler colours. A cityscape on the red length shows what may be Beijing with aspirational skyscrapers, while the blue length shows what seems to be either a thundering waterfall, rather like Niagara, or perhaps the Yangtze Gorges. This iconography is specific to the period of economic reform instigated by China's leader Deng Xiaoping (1904–97) from 1978. The then still unbuilt skyscrapers are the visible sign of the 'Four Modernizations' that were the central pillar of Deng's regime. The gorges of the Yangtze River, if that is indeed what this cotton length shows, stand both for the beauty of China's landscape, long a focus of communist imagery, and also for the proposed project to dam the mighty river for its hydroelectric potential.

47 Two lengths of printed cotton
*c.*1978
200 x 73 cm
V&A: FE.14 and
FE.15-1994
Given by Clio Whittaker

48 Women of the Miao nationality buying cotton prints
*c.*1960
This photograph is taken from a Beijing publication celebrating the communes of Mao's China, *People's Communes*, edited by the Ministry of Agriculture, People's Republic of China (Peking: Foreign Languages Press, 1960), unpaginated.

Before describing how people deployed textiles on walls and floors, we will consider the possibility that some of the V&A's textiles were originally set into frames and used as panels for screens. Several silk pieces described elsewhere in this book have, or are known to have had, wooden frames, although it is by no means only textiles that form screen panels. A variety of materials, as well as a diversity of sizes and shapes, exist and these moveable items of furniture can change the layout of a space, form a grand backdrop to a seated person, keep out drafts and generally add interest to a Chinese room. Folding screens from China are the most commonly seen kind in the West and foreigners were attracted to them from the seventeenth century, when colourful incised lacquer screens first reached Europe.[9] Much later, westerners resident in China in the early years of the twentieth century commissioned carved, black wooden frames specially for the silk tapestry pictures that were coming onto the antiques market at that time and which were acquired as seventeenth-century examples of the silk weaver's art.[10] Such a set of pictures came to the museum from the daughter of a Belgian diplomat.

Two of the pictures, from a group of eight in the V&A, are shown here (plate 49). It is difficult to date them, although they are perhaps not so early as originally thought. At the top of each panel, Guanyin, the Goddess of Mercy, the feminized Chinese version of the Buddhist bodhisattva Avalokiteshvara, dispenses deliverance from worldly perils. On the left she protects the supplicant from shipwreck, while on the right she causes an attacker's sword to shatter into fragments. These stories of earthly redemption ultimately depend on the text known as the *Guanyin Sutra*, itself originally a chapter in the longer *Lotus Sutra*, a key scripture of the Buddhist canon.[11] Although eight is a usual number for panels in a folding screen, it should not be presumed that they were made for such a piece of furniture or that the set is complete. Guanyin has many personifications. We may not know exactly how they were displayed by their original Chinese owner but these Buddhist pictures seem likely to have been for devotional use at home.

Other panel-shaped tapestry lengths in the museum are made from two or three small pictures sewn together, and this disposition, with scenes of figures or flowers enclosed within a frame one on top of another, is seen on Chinese cabinets and

49 Panels of tapestry woven silk
1600–1900
102 x 22 cm
V&A: T.269-1971

cupboards from the late nineteenth century.[12] The museum also has a number of single unmounted silk tapestry pictures with various groupings of flowers, insects and antiques. The majority have blue grounds, although some have brown and a few have gold (plate 50). The designs line up one with another, along the same axis, when the pieces are placed side by side. Although the tapestry technique theoretically allows the back to be indistinguishable from the front, a mass of thread ends disfigures the reverse of these pictures.

On some of the pieces there are stitch, tack or adhesive markings, which are suggestive of their having been mounted in screens, although it is not altogether implausible that they could have been mounted in albums. The representations on these silk pictures correspond with coloured woodblock prints first produced in the seventeenth century, although this does not mean that the small panels also date from that time. No totally convincing thesis as regards their age has been put forward.[13] What can be said at the present time is that the comparable recorded pieces in Chinese collections are, on close inspection, rather different from the ones that are preserved outside China.[14] Because so many of them seem to be in the West, there is a possibility that there was a revival of the tapestry technique, called *kesi* in Chinese, in the nineteenth and twentieth centuries, when workshops survived by producing articles for foreign residents and visitors. The earliest date that one of these pictures was acquired by the V&A is 1901.

A more plausible candidate for an album leaf is the picture in plate 51.[15] Against a cream ground, a small bird with soft brown, yellow and grey plumage opens its beak to sing. It sits on the branch of a camellia-like shrub, which blooms with red and pink flowers. Formerly displayed in the V&A as coming from the Song dynasty (960–1279) or the early Ming dynasty (1368–1644), and recorded in the museum inventory as from the Ming dynasty, the date of its manufacture is perhaps still open to rather more speculation than the certainty expressed in the records might suggest. While it undoubtedly depends on a style of bird and flower painting that has its ultimate origins in the court culture of the Song period, these conventions, disseminated more widely through the medium of print culture, remained vital over a long span of China's later imperial history and are visible in a wide array of luxury craft products.

This piece is mounted in a Chinese card folder covered in white patterned silk, and the four brushed characters to the right of the frame read *song* ('Song dynasty'), *xiu* ('embroidery'), *hua* ('flower') and *niao* ('bird'). The frame and label are certainly not from the Song or Ming periods. Pictures in this format were not designed for permanent display, but the albums that contained them were the subjects of occasional connoisseurly scrutiny, often in a social context. Paintings of the Ming and Qing dynasties depict men and sometimes women showing and commenting on such albums in affluent domestic or garden settings.

Wallpaper was not a native Chinese tradition of interior decoration despite a brisk trade in painted paper panels from south China to Europe from the 1690s. Walls in Chinese rooms were, however, sometimes decorated with different types of textile. Many of these are considered in the next chapter, for most were only put up temporarily, as

50 Album leaf or screen panel of tapestry woven silk
1750–1920
43.9 x 28.6 cm
V&A: T.104-1948
Vuilleumier Collection, purchased with a grant from the National Art Collections Fund

51 Album leaf of tapestry woven silk
1600–1800
30.6 x 25 cm
V&A: T.232-1948
Vuilleumier Collection, purchased with a grant from the National Art Collections Fund

52 Wall hanging of tapestry
woven silk
*c.*1850–1900
93 x 103 cm
V&A: T.72-1914
Given by Charles Lund

occasion demanded. The ones discussed here sometimes give obvious hints as to the
private or public observances their display marked, but they can also be viewed as part of
the total interior setting.

A particular style of hanging (plate 52), of which the V&A has several examples, is
hard to place in its social context, although like the table frontals that it resembles in
several ways it is composed of three main pieces of cloth. When hung on a wall, the
distinctive curved section might have framed and highlighted an image. Like the
embroidered table frontal discussed above (pages 41 and 42), this one follows the
convention of *san lan*, literally 'three blues', a favoured colour combination of the late
nineteenth and early twentieth centuries, which uses several tones of blue and white to
the exclusion of other shades. The design of fantasy butterflies and flowers, and the blue
theme, are continued across the pelmet. Wall hangings like this are woven to shape. This
means that, although the three sections were sewn together later, the two silk-patterned
pieces came off the loom with integral borders and an outline that was already
recognizable as the finished article.

This method of tapestry weaving was standard practice in China for traditional
clothing and it is from garments woven this way, but never fully tailored, that we can
gain an insight into the techniques used for such interior decorations (page 104). The
implications for cost of this method of production have yet to be understood, but it can
be assumed that these tapestry-woven furnishings were on the pricey side.

A pair of pictures from the late eighteenth century, one of which is shown here (plate 53) is also for decorating the walls of a room. The technique used for the picture is accomplished embroidery rather than tapestry. It portrays the Royal Mother of the West, attended by two graceful fairy maids who fan her and carry aloft a tray of longevity peaches respectively. At her feet is a phoenix bird. The composition of the picture is given some depth by the expanse of dark blue ground wreathed in cloud trails and, despite being faded and worn, the stitches, which are worked with decorative overlays and in different directions, still appear glossy. The shape of the picture holds the eye and it can be seen that the line of the embroidery work fits the outline of the wooden frame at the bottom and sides.

It is likely that the shape of the picture echoed that of other pieces of furniture in the room, the entire contents of which were probably designed to order. From 1750, the moneyed elite thought it chic to put glass over the fronts of their pictures, although the surviving glass over these V&A pieces is not from the eighteenth century and must have been renewed over the years. The wooden frames and metal hangers are contemporary with the embroideries. There is more visual evidence for the use of such framed pictures from the end of the nineteenth century and beginning of the twentieth century than there is for earlier periods.[16]

A vertical scroll from the last decades of the nineteenth century (plate 54) is a typical example of the kind of fine embroidery work that enjoyed a flowering at this time. It depicts a willow tree with a peony flower growing at its base. Swallows, a kingfisher poised as if ready to dive and a pair of cranes complete the composition. Like Chinese

53 Framed and embroidered silk picture
1730–1800
64.9 x 105.4 cm
V&A: T.355-1970

scroll paintings, it probably would not have hung permanently on the wall, but was brought out at certain seasons and admired for a while. This type of picture is therefore very much a part of the interior design scheme of a well-off household. Such embroideries were not to be dismissed as second-rate paintings, for the challenges of creativity were rather differently inflected in China before the twentieth century. This piece is embroidered from an original painting by Yun Shouping (1633–90), a renowned bird and flower painter, and then copied by Lü Shi, whose name and that of the studio, together with a stanza of poetry and Lü Shi's red seal mark, are all worked in embroidery stitches to the left of the scroll. The embroiderer remains anonymous. That this scroll is after a painting is not to its detriment. The fact that it is 'painted' with silk threads is evidence that it is not a slavish copy but rather a wholly acceptable way of honouring the original artist. 'Original' and 'reproduction' were not seen as opposites.[17]

One of the pioneers of Chinese art scholarship, Stephen Bushell (1844–1908), writing in 1904, called this scroll an example of 'Canton work'.[18] It is from this period particularly that commentaries about Chinese embroidery centred on the execution and recognition of distinct regional styles. These styles seem to have emanated from professional studios that reached out to a defined audience of middle-class buyers both Chinese and foreign.

A final, late surge of imperial patronage renewed interest in embroidery and enabled the craft to develop during the twentieth century. In 1904 the Dowager Empress Cixi (1835–1908) commissioned work from the embroiderer Shen Shou (1874–1921), who went on to become internationally famous. Through her subsequent teaching and writing, Shen Shou championed and promoted the embroidery arts. One of her first commissions for Cixi was a hanging scroll with swallows among the weeping branches of a willow tree, very much in the same vein as the V&A's scroll. Her later work tended to move away from this traditional format, and this new embroidery movement, encouraged by other serious practitioners besides Shen Shou, resulted in pictures like the seascape shown in plate 55.[19]

The picture-making possibilities of the embroidery technique have been stretched to the limits on this virtuoso piece. It is worked with enormous care and skill, although we do not know the name of the embroiderer. The design elements of the central wave, with two sailing boats on the far horizon balanced by a pair of diving gulls to the right, are embroidered in a limited palette of greys and blues and white. The seascape is built up of tiny straight stitches that are packed into the design area, leaving the top of the background silk as an empty sky. The date of the piece is uncertain, but it can be placed somewhere between 1910 and 1940. Glazed and framed, it might have graced the walls of a contemporary-style home.

The carpet shown in plate 56 was also made in China during the period 1910 to 1940, although its abstract design aesthetic is rather different from that of the romantic seascape. There was a brief flowering of inventive rug making in the

54 Embroidered silk scroll
1860–80
160 x 43 cm
V&A: 1864-1888

55 Embroidered silk seascape
*c.*1910–40
48.3 x 67.3 cm
V&A: T.119-1963

cities of Beijing and Tianjin in these years, although as early as 1904 contemporary Chinese rugs were well received at the St Louis Exposition in North America.

Owing to the loss of markets in Turkey during the First World War (1914–18), carpet import and export enterprises in America and Europe turned to China to satisfy the needs of interior designers. It was a time of cooperation between western entrepreneurs and Chinese businesses producing modernist patterns for fashionable interiors.[20] Although many of the pieces were destined for the West, they were also used in the individually designed houses of Chinese people, as well as in the skyscraper hotels and office buildings that came to dominate the Shanghai waterfront at this time.

The piece shown here is a key example of the genre. It displays the technical features characteristic of Chinese-produced carpets of the period, as well as the distinctive palette of chrome green. What makes it a particularly significant purchase, however, is the design. Although the V&A has identified a carpet in its collection (V&A T.296-1977) by the British designer Betty Joel (1896–1985) as having been woven in China in the 1930s, the piece under consideration successfully combines the Chinese traditional with the modern.

This synthesis was advocated by Chinese design theorists keen to encourage contemporary practitioners to rediscover and utilize China's own artistic heritage in their work, rather than look to the West for cultural styles. For this reason, we believe that the striking trio of central motifs on this carpet, echoing archaic bronze and jade patterns, was drafted by a Chinese designer with this adaptation of forms in mind. A notable figure in this respect is Chen Zhifo (1895–1962), whose compilations of several volumes of examples of Chinese designs from historic sources, plus his own graphic work, influenced designers in the 1920s and 30s.[21]

56 Carpet, wool pile
*c.*1930
254 x 175.3cm
V&A: FE.2-2003
Purchased with a grant
from the Donor Friends
of the V&A

57 Carpet, wool pile
1870–1900
211 x 444.5cm
V&A: T.2-1936
Given by E. Guy Ridpath

At the present time the designer of this carpet cannot be identified with any certainty, although it is hoped that further research in as yet untapped Chinese sources of the period will provide more positive clues. The political events in China during the late 1920s and on through the 1930s and 40s prevented artist designers from realizing their work into tangible objects. This distinctive carpet represents one of the few designs that came to fruition in these conflicted times.

Although an unusual shape, another pile carpet (plate 57) has a more predictable design arrangement and colour. It has been suggested that this type of patterning was dictated by European fashion but, like the modernist rug, it could have fitted equally well into a Chinese or western interior from the time it was made in the late nineteenth or early twentieth century. Its several borders and medallion decorations, and its all-over scattering of traditional motifs, flowers and fruits, represent an often-repeated formula. It resembles several other pieces in the collection that were acquired by the museum in 1909.[22]

These carpets are the descendants of a northwestern heritage of rug making that began to spread eastwards in the 1860s. While Inner Mongolia and the provinces of Ningxia and Gansu, all wool-producing regions, continued manufacturing carpets, skills from these areas were introduced to Beijing and Tianjin. In 1872, for example, a carpet-weaving school was established in Beijing under imperial auspices and headed by a Buddhist monk from Gansu.[23] We have seen how, later on, in the first half of the twentieth century, these kinds of initiatives resulted in fruitful partnerships between Chinese and foreign firms in China's eastern cities. While rugs with 'deco' patterning are often not recognized as Chinese, those with patterns perceived to be at the more traditional end of the design spectrum have received special attention from collectors. Chinese carpets are subjected to the same evaluation process that connoisseurs apply to 'oriental carpets' of all kinds when

58 Two bolts of patterned silk
*c.*1900–1910
Silver and black
V&A: T.141-1927
411 x 76.2 cm
Given by T.B. Clarke-Thornhill
Gold and black
V&A: T.176-1937
426 x 73.6 cm
Griffith Bequest
In memory of General
Sir J. Ronald Leslie MacDonald
The inscriptions on the loom
ends tell us that both bolts were
made in Nanjing. They give the
names of the shops which
marketed them.

judging them for those two most covetable but elusive qualities, age and authenticity. This has led to some fanciful and misguided attributions.[24]

We began this chapter by looking at two unused lengths of silk. These bolts constitute a fairly large group within the V&A. Some of them at least should be considered as complementing the painterly artistic output of traditional China. Although elite painters increasingly utilized paper as their material of choice after the fifteenth century, the mounting and protection of painted screens, scroll paintings, album leaves and precious secular and religious books was dependent on different speciality silks. Painted scrolls and printed books in the V&A's collection provide an idea of the types of silk used and the ways they were employed. It seems likely that some of the museum's silks may have been destined for such purposes. For example, the early twentieth-century bolts with gold and silver geometric designs shown in plate 58 are the kinds of material used for the ends of one particular type of scroll roller.[25]

4 CHINESE TEXTILES FOR SPECIAL OCCASIONS

In their original Chinese settings, many decorative textiles now in the Victoria and Albert Museum were used to transform both domestic and sacred spaces on specific occasions. Some were specially commissioned for particular situations from professional workshops; others were the result of more homely endeavours.

Several of the pieces in the collection bear names and dates, but their precise contexts elude us and their dispersal has severed them from their past. Though the purposeful impetus behind each textile's creation cannot now be recaptured, taken together they bear witness to some of the powerful traditional values held by Chinese people and, in the post-1949 communist era, to the political ideology that permeated their lives. Such textiles intensified the festivals, religious ceremonies and family rituals that punctuated the daily routine of the Chinese year. They communicated meanings in visual form.[1]

China is famous for the splendid textiles that were bestowed on the dead.[2] There are few such textiles in the V&A, and those that do have an association with death are mourning garments for the living. In contrast, celebratory hangings, connected with the affirmation of life, form a large group within the collection. These are mostly figurative pieces adorned with sets of recurring images that dominated textile design, as well as other Chinese decorative arts, from the late eighteenth century to the twentieth century.

Many of these silks were stitched or woven onto a red ground. Chinese rituals are traditionally divided into *bai shi* and *hong shi,* 'white occasions' and 'red occasions', that is mourning and celebrating, hence the red on many of the V&A pieces. Several have netted and tasselled fringes. The hangings are of different shapes and sizes, and most are large as befits pieces to be displayed on family or public occasions. Many were made to celebrate birthdays and weddings, two universal rites of passage that consolidate an individual's place in the world.

A striking set of twelve panels, two of which are shown here (plates 59 and 60), is from the nineteenth or twentieth century. Some of the panels bear inscriptions providing a glimpse of the people involved in this particular anniversary. The set was made for Mrs Gao on her eightieth birthday and we learn that she was an *an ren*, literally 'a peaceful person', but here an honorific title granted to wives of public officials of the sixth rank. The embroideries were presented by a nephew, Wu Shiyuan, who chose the theme of filial piety as an appropriate homage to his elderly aunt. The narrative embroidery depicts all twenty-four examples of filial piety, a canon of stories with a complex history that seems to have been codified in the Han dynasty (206 BC–AD 220), although its sentiments reach further back in Chinese history to the time of Confucius in the sixth century BC. Those who revered their parents and elders and, by extension, their

rulers, had been praised by China's great philosophical sage. This ideal of respect came to form a cornerstone of traditional Chinese society, and stories circulated of those who went to extremes in order to honour their elders. The tales became so much part of the fabric of Chinese culture, with generations of children being inculcated with their message, that the pictures alone were instantly recognizable.

The top of the panel with the dedicatory inscription from Mrs Gao's nephew depicts the story of the fourteen-year-old Yang Xiang, who sacrificed his own life by throwing himself under the claws of a tiger that was attacking his father. The tiger's jaunty red ears and sequin eyes somewhat dilute the story's grim subject matter, but the father's lost hat, blown off in the rush to escape, injects a touch of panic into the scene. Below is the story of the impoverished Jiang Ge, who fled from a troubled land carrying his widowed mother on his back. Despite many ensuing deprivations, he continued to provide for her. The detail in another panel shows a loyal son, Yan, disguised as a deer in order to go among the herd and get milk for his ailing mother. At the beginning of the twentieth century these moral tales were known to some English speakers through the popular 'Wisdom of the East' series, published by John Murray. *The Book of Filial Duty* came out in 1908.

Another aunt whose name has not come down to us was the recipient of the long crimson panel from the nineteenth century shown in plate 61. It depicts four of the 'Eight Immortals', semi-mythical personages who were originally associated with Daoism, China's native religion. These figures of good luck and longevity are sometimes seen separately and sometimes together. They are frequently grouped in two sets of four, so there may have been a companion panel to this one showing the other Immortals and perhaps giving the aunt's name and age. We know that a person who attained the age of sixty in China was especially venerated because they had lived through a complete cycle of the Chinese calendar.[3] The inscription on the surviving piece reads: 'Your loving nieces, Zhou Yingchun and Zhou Mingsheng, together bow their heads and offer congratulations'. The robes, clouds and characters are filled in with metallic foil in two tones of gold and one of silver

A set of four scrolls, one of which (plate 62) is pictured here, seems to record another birthday. They appear to have a connection with the Dowager Empress Cixi (1835–1908), a forceful and reactionary ruler who effectively held power in China from 1861 until her death. This scroll, like the other three, has her seal at the centre top. The embroidery shows a red-crested crane and peony flowers, associated with a long life and royalty respectively. All four scrolls are very likely to have been embroidered from paintings made by the empress herself and embroidered by court artisans for the all-important sixtieth birthday of Cixi. This occurred in 1894, the equivalent of the date recorded on this set. The scrolls were perhaps distributed as gifts as part of the lavish birthday celebrations.[4]

Another birthday hanging (plate 63) is a distinct kind of celebratory textile that employs writing as almost the only form of decoration. Like many V&A textiles it dates from the end of the Qing dynasty (1644–1911). Here, the 'writing' instrument is a needle instead of a brush, and the technique is one of filling in a pre-painted outline. The metallic threads are laid down on the surface of the background silk within the

62 Embroidered silk
birthday scroll
Dated 1894
185.4 x 43.2 cm
V&A: T.76-1971

63 Birthday hanging, silk with
couched gold embroidery
1850–1900
240 x 174 cm
V&A: T.214-1962
Given by Mrs Campbell Coffin

64 Embroidered silk
birthday hanging (detail)
1850–1900
51.5 x 337.8 cm
V&A: T.21-1911
Given by Mr A.E. Anderson

framework of the characters. They are kept in place by stitches worked across the bulky gold and taken through to the reverse.

The ability to write characters well, and to comprehend their meaning, has a central place in Chinese culture. The educated invested large amounts of time learning characters, and even those regarded as illiterate understood the rudiments of the system. Everyone, from whichever part of the empire they came, would recognize the central character on this hanging as *shou,* meaning 'long life'. Household servants present at the birthday reception would have understood the significance of the other characters too, even though they could not read them.

Hung in a prominent position on the occasion of the recipient's birthday this piece was not itself the present but rather the gift tag or birthday card. The 'long-life' character, frequently co-opted into the Chinese decorative repertoire in the late Qing period, is surrounded by other, smaller characters which reveal that the piece was commissioned by a son-in-law for a father-in-law, a man in the sixth rank of the Civil Service called Tan Shanpu. His substantive title, as well as the honorific that goes with it, are embroidered after his name, along with his wife's and his concubine's name and the honorific titles for these two women. There is no indication as to which birthday is being honoured. No date is included in the respectful inscription, which is mostly taken up with lists of the other donors, namely all the sons-in-law and grandsons of Mr Tan. The recipient therefore seems to have had only daughters, and the grandson name lists seem to suggest that one of the sons-in-law is deceased. Given that men in gentry families did not marry until they were twenty years old, and that grandchildren would not be regarded as mature enough to be included in such an inscription before they were thirteen or so years of age, it seems likely that Mr Tan would be celebrating at least his sixtieth birthday.

A story frequently encountered on birthday hangings is the uplifting tale known as 'A Tableful of Honours' (*Man chuang hu*, literally 'court tablets'). It relates the visit home of successful sons and sons-in-law to attend the sixtieth birthday celebrations of General Guo Ziyi of the Tang dynasty (AD 618–906). It is found on several of the V&A's pieces, two of which are illustrated here (plates 64 and 65). The detail shows an elderly couple sitting in front of a screen emblazoned with different versions of the character for longevity, while the very large crimson hanging has the story as its central tableau. This particular birthday hanging, which includes a date equivalent to 1863, is divided into several sections filled with figures and lucky motifs, as well as a long inscription. This identifies both the recipient, Mr Huang, a native of Guangdong province, who was celebrating his ninetieth birthday, and a host of well wishers.

The splendid silk panel is beautifully designed and executed. Each area of decoration is marked off from its neighbour by a repeating border and the whole composition is held together by a limited palette of blue, green and gold embroidery against a crimson satin ground (plates 66 and 67). The material quality of the piece is enhanced by streamers, attached at the top but otherwise floating freely, decorated with a traditional good-luck message in characters embroidered in a style known as seal script.

For the donor of the hanging, Mrs Stewart Lockhart, its original context of production and consumption in late Qing China was of less interest than another facet of its subsequent biography. This was its use, in 1934, in the first production of one of the theatrical sensations of the day, S.I. Hsiung's play *Lady Precious Stream*. This Chinese-style drama was a tremendous success on the London stage in an era of revived enthusiasm for chinoiseries of all kinds, and coincidentally brought together a number of key cultural luminaries of twentieth-century China. In addition to the writer himself, these included the painter Xu Beihong (1895–1953), who provided watercolour illustrations to the published text of the play, and the acclaimed actor Mei Lanfang (1894–1961), who was in London at the time.

Mei's presence in London was part of a highly influential tour in which he was nonetheless unsuccessful in putting his more authentic brand of Chinese stage practice before the British public. He is known to have attended a reception at which the donor of the hanging was also present. The Bohemian social circles in which Mei Lanfang moved also included such notable sojourners in London as the Chinese American film star Anna May Wong (1905–61) and the singer and activist Paul Robeson (1898–1976), himself known to James Laver (1899–1975), a high-profile V&A curator with a wide circle of contacts and one of the museum's early enthusiasts for the study of dress.[5]

The hanging was given a strong canvas lining and black tape ties across the top to facilitate its display as part of the set dressing for *Lady Precious Stream* – a setting very different from that for which it was originally created. This and a companion piece from the same source dated to 1846 are thought to have been purchased by the donor's father James Stewart Lockhart (1858–1937), who negotiated the expansion of Hong Kong into the New Territories from a Chinese merchant family there in 1879.[6]

In China, images of boys are pervasive throughout the decorative arts of the last 1,000

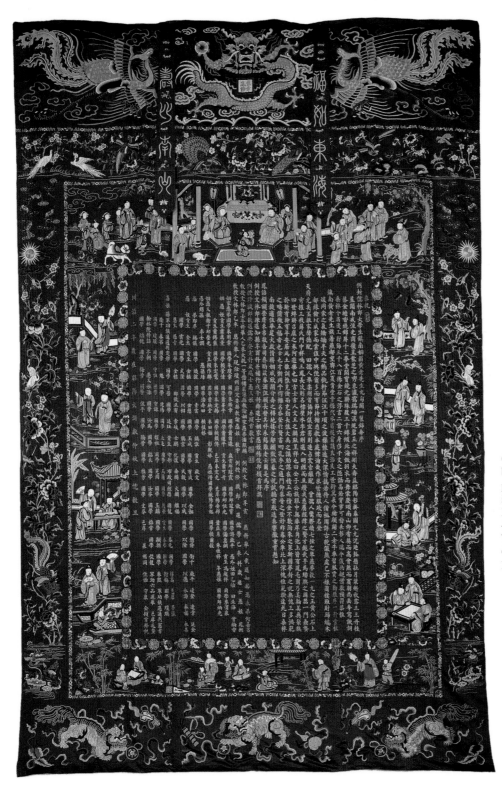

65 Embroidered silk
birthday hanging with
painted dedicatory
inscription
Dated 1863
436.9 x 250 cm
V&A: T.159-1964
Given by Mrs Stewart
Lockhart

66 Embroidered silk birthday hanging (border detail of plate 65) Gentleman playing the *qin*

67 Embroidered silk birthday hanging (border detail of plate 65) Gentlemen and servant with flowers

years. On the early-nineteenth-century wedding textile in plate 68 they are depicted carrying lanterns, pulling along a toy animal on wheels and flying fish kites. Children are frequently depicted engaging in pleasurable activities in such idyllic settings. Family groups are rare before the advent of photography and, with few exceptions, children are shown free from adult supervision. This seeming freedom should not be construed as a validation of Rousseau-like innocence, however, for these images serve the needs of the adult world. Duty, service and respect, differently inflected over a long period of China's history right up to the modern era, are the messages of these kinds of pictures.

Representations of childhood flowered during the Song period (960–1279) with poets also taking up the theme. By the Ming period (1368–1644), and more especially the Qing, depictions of boys in paintings and woodblock prints, and on lacquer, ceramics and particularly textiles, became ubiquitous. Noteworthy are two sumptuously embroidered jackets from the coffin of the Xiaojing empress (d.1612), a wife of the Wanli emperor (r.1573–1620). Each is decorated with the 'hundred boys' design and shows the beautifully dressed children in a garden landscape playing with a variety of toys and animals, watching and acting in plays, or making music.[7]

The urgent need to secure the patrilineal line within the family, of whatever social strata, and to ensure that there would be a new male generation to perform the rites for the clan ancestors, made it imperative that wives should bear sons. Bed curtains and

68 Embroidered silk
picture (detail)
*c.*1800–1850
Whole picture 167.6 x 48.9 cm
V&A: T.446-1966
Given by Mr J.A. Blackwood

quilts for newly-weds were therefore decorated with *baizitu* ('pictures of a hundred boys') bearing wishes for many male offspring. The *baizitu* refers to an old Chinese story about the legendary king Zhou Wen Wang, who adopted an abandoned baby and thus increased his already large family of ninety-nine sons to a round hundred.[8] While such textiles rejoiced in male progeny, the compelling necessity to rear boys meant that daughters could be neglected or, worse, murdered at birth. As a consequence, males at times outnumbered females in the population, leaving many men single, rootless and unemployed, a condition concealed by these joyful visual manifestations of the fervent wish for sons.[9]

To increase the chance of a son's future prosperity and to ensure a suitable marriage alliance, families ardently hoped that their offspring would excel in the civil service examinations and secure a place in China's imperial bureaucratic hierarchy. A tasselled embroidered picture (plate 69) embodies this sentiment in the form of a *guizi*, a 'noble son'. He rides a green-scaled beast, known as a *qilin*. The auspicious credentials of this mythical one-horned creature cannot be bettered, for one legend tells of its appearance to the mother of Confucius, heralding the philosopher's birth. The boy astride the *qilin,* richly dressed in a voluminous robe, has a *ruyi*, a wish-granting sceptre, in one hand, and in the other a branch of *Osmanthus fragrans,* a flowering shrub native to west China and the Himalayan region. In reality, the powerfully scented flowers of the sweet or fragrant olive, as this osmanthus is called, are rather insignificant. Nonetheless, it is recognized as *guihua*, its Chinese name, which sounds the same as *guizi*, 'noble son', and is associated with literary success.

This auspicious boy on a *qilin* motif was used on silver charms shaped like locks that were worn around the necks of infant sons to protect them as children and secure prosperous lives for them when they grew up. So although this particular design, along with the colours green and red often used for baby clothes, are in some instances associated with the early years of Chinese childhood, this hanging from the late nineteenth century is not necessarily for a child. The motifs surrounding the boy and beast are appropriate to marriage, and the piece could well be a wedding mirror cover, used in a similar way to the Straits beaded hangings discussed below.[10]

In the Qing period especially, the iconography carrying wishes for a long and prosperous professional and family life was shared by all classes. Wealth, or the lack of it, might determine the type and style of picture making, but inexpensive woodblock prints bore similar motifs to costly carved lacquer pieces. Regional skills and materials made for other variations within a commonly held repertory of images.

The illustrated quilt cover (plate 70) was made in Fujian province and has been given

a date of between 1920 and 1940. It depicts one of the filial piety tales (page 56), here decorating an article for a bride's trousseau. In keeping with the sentiment of the occasion, the scene shows the presentation of a son, seen on a white horse, to a now-ennobled man who had earlier sold himself into bondage to pay for his father's funeral. Significantly, the man's freedom was secured by money earned from the sale of cloth woven by an immortal lady, which highlights the very real link, in the mortal world, between textiles and the contribution made by Chinese women to the household economy.

Although the imagery refers to a widely recognized story, this particular cover is an unusual and beautiful survival of the craft of stencilling and resist dyeing of Changle county, a coastal area of south China. Many Chinese emigrated to Java from this region and became involved in the Javanese batik industry. The close ties that these migrants maintained with their native place resulted in the exchange of technical innovations and design ideas between the two artisanal communities.

69 Embroidered silk
mirror cover
1880–1920
41.9 x 28.9 cm
plus 15.2 cm fringe
V&A: T.81-1968
Given by Miss M. Swallow

70 Cover for a quilt, cotton
with resist-dyed decoration
1920–40
181x 176 cm
V&A: FE.19-1984

71 Beadwork mirror cover
Straits Chinese
1900–1920
41.9 x 24.8 cm
V&A: T.48-1938
Given by Miss J. Gollan

72 Beadwork mirror cover
Straits Chinese
1900–1920
34.3 x 21.6 cm
V&A: T.49-1938
Given by Miss J. Gollan

The beadwork wedding panels (plates 71 and 72) also have a south-east Asian connection, probably coming from Penang and dating from the early years of the twentieth century. Each would form part of a cover used to drape over the front of a mirror in a bridal chamber. Reflecting surfaces are notorious in legend for holding the reflection of malignant spirits, so they are concealed as part of the marriage ritual to ensure a propitious start to the partnership. The story of artefacts like these is one of community identification, interaction and assimilation. They originate from Chinese families who live in what is today Malaysia, and who during the nineteenth century and first three decades of the twentieth century forged a highly distinctive culture that bore traces both of their original homeland and of the Malay region where they settled. Furthermore, aspects of European life were blended with this mixture, for the period of this culture's greatest flowering coincided with British colonial rule in the area, then known as the British Straits Settlements of Penang, Singapore and Malacca. 'Straits-born Chinese', one of the names for these south-east Asian settlers, were businessmen, bankers and government functionaries who mostly looked askance at manual work while enjoying its fruits. Straits women, with unbound feet and given the honorific title Nonya or Nyonya, were the stewards of material culture and the transmitters of taste.[11]

Beading and embroidery were the only handicrafts executed by the Straits Chinese themselves, and even then only small items were made in the domestic sphere; large hangings and wedding outfits, along with Straits china, gold, silverware and furniture, were ordered from professionals outside the home, often from south China. Girls learned the sewing techniques from their mothers and grandmothers.

Although weddings and the celebrations and rituals surrounding the nuptials were manifestations of the Chinese roots of the Straits-born, the beading technique does not have its origins in China. It began to flourish at a time when large-scale European manufacture of small glass beads was perfected in the nineteenth century. The threaded work that comprises these pieces relies solely on cotton thread and small beads with no backing material. The technique is painstaking in the extreme. The piece with a central vase containing a rose-like peony, a favourite flower of Straits communities, has a red and white border showing the inventive use of differently sized beads. The fringe, too, includes larger and longer faceted orange beads with an iridescent coating. Both panels show a mix of transparent and milky opaque beads.[12]

Like Straits beadwork, Chinese cross-stitch embroideries (plates 73, 74 and 75) were made by women at home in preparation for weddings. Unlike the Straits pieces, however, the two-colour cottons were produced within the boundaries of the Chinese mainland. There are around thirty examples of these blue on white, or sometimes black on white, embroideries in the museum's collection, all dating from the beginning of the twentieth century. They pose some intriguing questions, representing as they do a different cloth tradition from the one of silk that came to dominate the V&A's collecting policy for Chinese textiles. What are the factors that contributed to that difference? Are they relevant to region, social class or the technique itself? All of these are theoretically possible, and all present reasonable avenues of enquiry. The present state of our knowledge does not permit a definite resolution of these issues, although the embroideries themselves and the circumstances of their acquisition give us partial answers.

Although there is a certain iconographic uniformity across the material culture of the Qing dynasty, one thing becomes clear when looking through the cross-stitch cottons. Some of the patterns that appear on them are not featured on other kinds of textiles. The square embroidery in plate 73 exhibits a design that is rarely if ever found elsewhere. The central scene depicts a game of dominoes, with all thirty-two tiles laid out in a specific

73 Embroidered cotton square
1880–1920
35 x 35 cm
V&A: Circ. 345-1927
Given by Miss Mary Lumsden

74 Embroidered cotton valance
1880–1920
45.7 x 182.9 cm
V&A: T.123-1927
Given by Miss Mary Lumsden

formation. The skill in playing depends on the ability to quote a certain reference when a particular combination of tiles is turned up. Amid the tiles sit four figures, each holding out a square tile marked with four pips, although the tile patterns seem to be whimsical and do not represent a normal set.[13]

The characters that form a cross in the centre can be deciphered as 'the three stars of happiness (*fu*), prosperity (*lu*), longevity (*shou*)'. The fact that the characters are reversed as in a mirror image is a visual pun between *dao*, 'to reverse', and *dao*, 'to arrive', indicating the advent of these three highly desired qualities in Chinese life. It may well be that these cotton embroideries provide some evidence of an alternative, now-vanished catalogue of designs that had currency before the visual world of late-imperial China became homogenized. Other designs on them have been linked to those on New Year pictures (*nianhua*), widely available woodblock prints mass produced for the festive season, and to papercuts that themselves sometimes serve as actual templates for embroidered textiles.[14]

The cross-stitch cottons were used for household linen, clothing and accessories; in recent years such embroideries have been seen covering the bride's face at weddings. The horizontal piece illustrated here (plate 74) is a bed valance. These valances hang along one side of the bed, reaching to the floor, or else are attached around the top. Roundels spaced along the cotton strip (plate 75), and borders carefully turned at the corners and defining the horizontal and vertical edges, are the standard features of such valances. Those here show a sure needlework hand and exemplify the clever incorporation of the white ground as an integral part of the design.

Embroideries like these are recorded as coming from several provinces in west China. The V&A's pieces came into the museum between 1920 and 1950, a significant time span for the collecting of such embroideries. This was a period of intense European interest in peasant needlework and in the deciphering of perceived symbolic meanings inscribed on such folk art.[15] It was also a time when many westerners were posted to west China to open the Burma Road, act as aid workers, set up cooperatives and teach. These educated foreigners were drawn to the embroideries because the values embodied in such handwork were believed to hold the clue to a better society in an age of fast-changing mores. The American anthropologist Carl Schuster (1904–69) travelled to this region of China specifically to collect embroideries like these.[16]

There was also at this same time an upsurge in the study of folklore by Chinese scholars, some of whom were trying to forge a national style of literature, art and design. Chinese academics and folklorists were forced to move further westwards because of the prevailing political situation in China during the years of the Japanese occupation (1937–45), and this naturally encouraged the study of local crafts. Fast disappearing in the first half of the twentieth century, these blue and white cross-stitch cottons do not seem to have enjoyed as great a revival as some other indigenous textiles in China, particularly those from China's so-named 'minority peoples'. An inferior type of work in the form of small, sparsely decorated cross-stitched souvenirs survived both before and after the communist victory in 1949.

Even though a woman occupied a subordinate position in traditional China, recent scholarship has determined several ways in which Chinese women, for the most part

75 Embroidered cotton valance (detail)
1880–1920
Whole valance 34.3 x 182.9cm
V&A: T.125-1927
Given by Miss Mary Lumsden
A large fish, perhaps a carp, and what look like a pair of cats dominate this roundel from a wedding valance. The carp carries the meaning of fertility because it lays many eggs. The cats, if that is what they are, can be read as 'twin happiness'.

consigned to silence, sought to subvert male domination. We have seen how they might retain a measure of control, on behalf of the family, over those textiles that played a crucial role in betrothal arrangements. An autonomy was possibly achieved by living in separate quarters to men, and a certain amount of female solidarity may arguably have been derived from sewing accomplishments.

A large nineteenth-century hanging embroidered with a dramatic tableau (plate 76) gives us an inkling of how women created a space for themselves in a patriarchal society. The celestial maiden flying down through the clouds on a dragon is the Weaver Girl who, by the patterns she weaves, has the power to influence the fate of humankind. For

76 Embroidered women's
festival silk hanging
*c.*1740–1820
155 x 140 cm
V&A: FE.114-1974
Given by Joan Evans

all but one night of each year she is separated from her lover, the Herd Boy, by a river of stars. Only when magpies make a bridge across the Milky Way is she able to cross over and be with him. Significantly, this part of the fable is not indicated here and no males appear on this celebration silk. To one side is the moon, depicted as a palace room, inside which are the female deity Chang'e and a charming white hare who tirelessly grinds at his mortar containing the elixir of life. On the other side, the mortal ladies inside the embroidery-hung pavilion play musical instruments, celebrating women's talents rather than their childbearing capacities. Those outside make obeisance to the Weaver Girl.

This hanging, possibly embroidered in the domestic sphere, does not match across the central seam and may once have been two separate banners. They were used at the Weaver Girl's Festival on the seventh day of the seventh month. The celebration, known as the 'Festival of Beseeching for Skills', was pointedly an all-female affair where the skills being sought were those connected with needlework. The occasion was often an excuse

77 Embroidered silk hanging with applied mirror decoration
Dated to the equivalent of 1827, 1887 or 1947
125 x 100 cm
V&A: T.149-1961

for intoxicated carousing, where ribald tales were told about the excluded males who otherwise so dominated their lives.[17]

While all celebratory textiles are understood as propitious in that they embody good wishes for the future, the tasselled banner featured here (plate 77), incorporating costly gold thread, fur and circles of mirror, seems also to be affirming a man's already-secure position in the business community. While we do not know the precise nature of the occasion for which the banner was made, the large character in the middle translates as 'generalissimo' and the information on the pennants, flanking the main section, tells us the recipient was the director of a timber company. The presentation was made by a coterie of named firms and is dated using a system of sixty-year cycles, the most plausible dates for this piece being 1827, 1887 or 1947.

The male Confucian world of respect embodied in this banner is quite different from that depicted in another, equally showy piece (plate 78) dating to approximately the same time span. Here, the milieu is of martial heroes, whose images provide a contrasting view of Chinese masculinity. The dramatic history of the Three Kingdoms Period in the third century AD was familiar to wide audiences, including those not possessed of formal literacy, through the medium of the theatre. It is the conventions of stage practice, including costumes and make-up, which inform the repertoire of the scenes on this temple banner, and the connection is reinforced by the fact that drama of this type was a central element in religious festivals, designed to entertain the gods as much as their human devotees. The identification of this lively embroidery as a temple piece is made secure by the inscription 'beizi wang temple' (*beizi wang miao*), repeated four times in large black characters on the reverse across the red lining.

The practice of religious faith has stimulated the production of huge numbers of precious textiles. In China, the staging of a multitude of indigenous folk rituals, as well as the Confucian veneration of ancestors, the performance of Daoism and the observance of Buddhist rites, are all accompanied by decorated fabric.[18] Sometimes it clothes an icon or a human practitioner, an altar or a temple wall. Sometimes it takes the form of an offering from a devout believer, and sometimes it forms the focal point of an act of worship. This may be how the Buddhist embroidered picture (plate 79) was once employed.

A distinction can be drawn between the iconic and non-iconic uses of images. Iconic images like the one shown here not only bear a portrait of the sacred personage, but are also believed to provide a temporary dwelling for their spirit. A picture like this would be installed on an altar along with candles and flowers, and a table of offerings. Non-iconic

78 Embroidered and couched silk hanging
1850–1940
94 x 113 cm
V&A: FE.26-1971
Given by Miss B. Clapham

images, for example those that serve as illustrations to holy books, have a more didactic purpose.[19] Although the primary subject here is prominent and in a formal pose, both marks of an iconic status, the original context of this particular embroidery is lost, and it may have served several overlapping functions. What can be said is that this most lovely of images, rendered so skilfully in now very faded floss silk embroidery thread, depicts a manifestation of the Bodhisattva Avalokiteshvara, of particular importance to Tibetans from the seventh century AD.

The spiritual leader of one Tibetan lineage, the Dalai Lama, is considered to be a reincarnation of this bodhisattva. Tibetan Buddhism, which flourished in China as well as Tibet itself, generated a distinct form of iconography. Based on esoteric scriptures, the resulting images appear not in human form, but with many faces and arms. The splendidly costumed bodhisattva stands on a lotus flower against a halo of radiating hands. The mountainous and wooded landscape gives way to billowing clouds among which are six seated figures. When the picture was bequeathed to the museum in 1902, the robed worthies at the bottom were identified as the Dalai Lama and Panchen Lama, but this has still to be verified. It was also said to be dated to 1783. Despite a thorough

79 Buddhist embroidered
silk *thangka*
1770–1800
127 x 73.5 cm
V&A: 1479-1902
Roberts Bequest

80 Carpet, silk pile
1958
210 x 124 cm
V&A: FE.15-1991

conservation initiative undertaken in 1988, no trace of an inscription was found, although a date at the end of the eighteenth century is commensurate with the period of intense imperial patronage of Tibetan Buddhism by the Qianlong emperor (r.1735–96).[20] This piece may have come from a palace workshop because of its resemblance to other examples with a more secure provenance, though the workmanship does not quite match known palace pieces. The Chinese-style mounting has straight sides and is not sharply angled outwards at the bottom, as is the Tibetan custom. Marks to guide the embroiderer were revealed at the time of conservation, although the exact process by which artists designed and made such images is unknown.

A much later and at first sight entirely different kind of textile on closer inspection reveals certain continuities with the Buddhist picture discussed above (plate 80). Both make links between cultural patronage and state power and both are testimonies to the ways in which China's multi-ethnic character has been addressed by ruling elites from the Qing dynasty to the post-1949 regime of Mao Zedong.

This silk pile rug was made on the occasion of one of the social and political upheavals that Mao viewed as essential to keeping the revolutionary spirit alive. The Great Leap Forward (1958–61) aimed to energize the population to greater economic productivity. Following on a good harvest in the summer of 1958, communal agriculture was endorsed and expanded, although famine was to ensue soon after, and people were encouraged to contribute to steel quotas by producing steel locally in what proved to be totally inadequate backyard furnaces.

The aspirations of the campaign, which in retrospect caused immense suffering, are pictorially represented on this rug. The corner designs show, from top left clockwise, a bucket of molten metal, a wheatsheaf, bolls of cotton and a truck, possibly laden with steel. In the centre is the emblem of the People's Republic of China surrounded by doves, symbols of peace popularized by the exiled Spanish artist Pablo Picasso (1881–1973), who was an activist in the French Communist party during this period. Below, dancing on a green sward and circled by a garland of flowers, grapes and peaches, are representatives of the national minorities of the People's Republic. A soldier from the

81 Woven silk picture of the Nanjing Yangtze River Bridge
*c.*1968
41 x 80 cm
V&A: FE.14-1997
The completion of this bridge in 1968 was cause for huge orchestrated rejoicing. Here the red flags celebrate the opening, facilitating the first direct rail link between Beijing and Shanghai. 'The people, only the people, are the driving force behind world history' is the slogan painted on one of the bridge's buttresses.

People's Liberation Army plays the accordion, arguably the first global musical instrument and one equally associated with activist politics of extreme left and right. The V&A purchased this rug in 1991 from the Beijing Carpet Factory Number One, where it was made in 1958. It was presumably destined as a gift to 'foreign friends' or as a showpiece in a government department, but it seems never to have been donated to either and was retained by the factory, a memorial now to both hope and despair.[21]

In the same vein, although more widely distributed because of their mass-production techniques, the woven pictures in plates 81, 82, 83 and 84 were awarded to individuals for achievements at work or in the political sphere, and also given to visiting 'foreign friends'. In truth, the worlds of politics and work were inseparable at every level, and the giving and receiving of such motivational images was designed to reinforce this link. The pictures were woven together in a long line and only later cut into separate items. Pictures of Mao, whether printed, woven or embroidered, decorated the walls of private houses as well as public spaces.[22] All those shown here not only served as gifts on specific occasions, but also themselves depict particular occasions.

82 Woven silk picture of Chairman Mao
1966–76
40 x 27 cm
V&A: FE.28-1999
Given by Mr Gordon Barrass
Mao is here wielding a brush and writing 'Bombard the headquarters' on a 'big character poster', authorizing Red Guards to challenge the establishment at the start of the Cultural Revolution (1966–76).

83 Woven silk picture of
Chairman Mao
1966–76
40 x 27 cm
V&A: FE.36-1999
Given by Mr Peter Wain
This picture of the 73-
year-old Mao wearing a
bathrobe commemorates
his famous 1966 swim in
the Yangtze at Wuhan.

84 Woven silk picture of a
young Chairman Mao
1966–76
59.6 x 41.8 cm
V&A: FE.40-1999
Given by Mr Peter Wain
This famous image of Mao
as a youth, entitled
*Chairman Mao Goes to
Anyuan*, depicts the leader,
on a much-eulogized
occasion, striding
purposely forwards to lend
his support to the first
communist-led coal
miners' strike of 1921.

毛 主 席 去 安 源

一九二一年秋，我们伟大的导师毛主席去安源，象自点燃了安源的革命烈火。

参观红色安源留念

中国江西丝绸服装厂

5 CHINESE TEXTILES FOR CLOTHING

TEXTILE FABRIC CAN BE CUT AND PIECED TOGETHER into a variety of different forms with comparative ease, and tailors can utilize the fluidity of fabric to fashion clothing of astonishing complexity and beauty. The material from which clothes are made is the focus of this chapter.

The museum's Chinese textile collection includes bolts and lengths of cloth as well as garments. While drape and manipulation of the fabric play their parts in the history of Chinese dress, many clothes from China now in the Victoria and Albert Museum date from the nineteenth and twentieth centuries, when straight-seamed tailoring predominated. There were therefore surfaces on the backs and fronts of garments, unbroken by pleats or ruffles, which invited decoration. It was for this decoration, and the techniques that produced it, that museums like the V&A first collected textiles, whether in the form of clothes or furnishings.

For the periods before 1600, there are textile fragments in the collection that seem to have been used for clothing. The shape of a shoe toe or the curve of an armhole can sometimes be discerned. Several interesting and creative attempts have been made to reconstruct some of these early garments from similar archaeological remains in other collections.[1] It is still far from clear, however, what these early pieces originally looked like.

The earliest dateable whole garment in the museum's Chinese dress collection is a silk tapestry robe that glows with strong colours and has an ostentatious pattern woven across the surface (plate 85). The material was first made around 1600, although the robe itself was tailored later or altered over the years. The iconography of paired deer and longevity characters against a ground of meandering peony flowers signals a special fabric connected with a birthday. The spotted deer, called *lu* in Chinese, the same sound as the first part of the name Luxing, the God of Rank and Remuneration, are depicted in gold-ground circles that are part of the original weaving and not separately applied. The shoulders and sleeves are patched together, but here too the roundels are an integral part of the fabric.

The weavers watched the motifs appear on the loom as they plied their shuttles back and forth in the separate areas of colour. When the silk came off the loom, the design was complete; nothing was added with brush and ink as is sometimes the case with finer, small-scale silk tapestries.

This robe was taken apart for conservation in the 1980s. It proved impossible to piece it together in what might have been its original form during the late Ming dynasty (1368–1644). There was confirmation, however, that the front and back had been consciously woven to shape as a garment. In-fill of white plain weave tapering from hem

85 Robe of tapestry woven silk
*c.*1600
113 x 180 cm
V&A: FE.41-1985
Purchased with a grant donated
by Lady Garner

86 Dragon robe of
tapestry woven silk
1780–1850
154 x 194 cm
V&A: T.199-1948
Vuilleumier Collection,
purchased with a grant from the
National Art Collections Fund
This imperial robe is
distinguished from similar robes
worn by bureaucrats by its
yellow colouring and by the
patterning of twelve small
motifs within the standard
dragon-and-cloud layout.

87 Dragon robe of tapestry
woven silk (detail of plate 86)
Back hem section

to underarm was revealed at the sides, and despite an insertion
across the top of the shoulders, it can be concluded that the front
and back sections, both left and right, were originally woven in
one long piece (page 104). This is obvious from the evidence of
two very distinct hands at work on the loom on each of the two
sides running straight through from front to back. The design is
rotated 180 degrees at each length's midpoint so that the pattern
appears the correct way up when viewed from either back or
front. There are at least twenty-two different colours, as well as
gold, incorporated into this tapestry robe, and the weavers took
care to conceal any poorly dyed portions of thread by looping
them to the reverse of the material.

   Whether such a garment was ever meant to be worn or even
originally seamed together we cannot now be sure, for despite
great advances in the development of a money economy in China
during the late Ming, luxury silk textiles remained a sort of
currency. An inventory of the confiscated goods of a disgraced
Grand Secretary, Yan Song (d.1565), dated 1562, contains
14,331 lengths of cloth, many of which are clearly dress lengths
that were never made up. The silk storeroom operated as a bank

vault and also as a repository for gifts. A Grand Secretary would have maintained his network of relationships by bestowing appropriate presents such as silk textiles.[2] With regard to this particular silk tapestry style it may well be that textile lengths like these, with their prominent and distinctive colouring, were destined for a particular market, region or patron, the details of which are as yet unknown.

One of the most numerous types of clothing from China in the West in both public institutions and private hands are dragon robes from the Qing dynasty (1644–1911). These robes, which have a striped hem and a formulaic design of nine dragons among clouds, were worn by Chinese bureaucrats throughout the empire, as well as by successive emperors and other members of the ruling family. The imperial dragon robe pictured here (plates 86 and 87), dating to the late eighteenth or early nineteenth century, is just one example of the genre within the V&A. The robes came on to the market in large numbers after the fall of the imperial dynasty in 1911, when a republican government adopted different dress styles as a mark of new citizenship. The abiding fascination with ritual and status on the part of western observers of the Chinese scene goes some way to explain this pattern of collecting dragon robes. Furthermore, for acquisitive western owners these robes, like other textiles, represented a tangible connection, tenuous in most cases, with the Son of Heaven's imperial court.[3]

Dragon robe yardage in the form of several uncut and untailored garments gives us useful information about production methods. Perhaps more importantly for the history of collecting, however, it provides evidence that at least some dragon robes were specially to satisfy a market for souvenirs made after the end of dynastic rule. The V&A acquired several such pieces over the years (V&A T.227-1928, T.200-1948, T.216-1948). Some are embroidered on silk so flimsy that it is hard to see how they could possibly have withstood wear as garments.

A more substantial silk, often satin, is common for made-up embroidered robes, whether they are dragon robes for men or floral gowns for women. Three lengths of deep-blue embroidered velvet dating from the turn of the twentieth century are therefore unusual. One of the lengths is pictured in plate 88. Although the embroidery itself is familiar from other garments for Chinese women, being in smooth satin stitch and a knot stitch variation, it is rarer to find such a technique on a velvet ground. The cut pile of the velvet is not an ideal surface for decorative stitching but here the embroiderer has handled the bulky pile well and overcome any awkwardness. The embroidery itself delineates the outlines of the

88 Dress length of embroidered velvet
*c.*1900
111.1 x 60.3 cm
V&A: T.3-1914
Given by Mr J. Burnet Geake

garment. The length illustrated shows one half of the front and sleeve. The portion beneath the sleeve, which is cut away for tailoring, has been utilized to embroider a narrow collarband section. This can be cut out and applied around the neck. Owing to the density of the velvet pile, it would have made a rather stiff garment.

Just before the acquisition of this particular velvet yardage by the V&A, it was exhibited in a show of Chinese art at the Whitechapel Art Gallery in 1913. Established in 1901, this pioneering gallery in London's East End, situated away from the capital's grander art institutions, continues to stage an interesting mix of shows, and its broad remit over the years has included work with an international flavour. Although not the Whitechapel's first show to feature Chinese objects, the one in 1913 included 158 pieces of textile out of a total of just over 500 other artefacts. These are briefly described in the paperback catalogue that accompanied the show, with the textiles listed first. The exhibition, confidently called 'Chinese Art', eschewed traditional hierarchical distinctions by giving all materials an equal profile.[4]

From the early twentieth century, embroidery as a means of dress decoration gradually fell out of favour. Trimmings on women's gowns and their panelled skirts continued to be embroidered, as did wedding dresses, but the technique was not the paramount one for the main section of the upper garment. It largely fell into disuse on men's clothing too because dragon and court robes, the main types of embroidered clothes for men, were not worn after 1911.

An attractive length of pink silk featuring orchid plants in staggered bands, intended for a woman's jacket (plate 89), is a good example of this early twentieth-century aesthetic. While embroidered edgings might have framed a finished garment made from this material, the pink silk relied for its appeal on the flowers and swaying foliage woven across its surface.

The Addis Bequest of 1983 includes great quantities of Chinese silk for clothes and the majority of them have monochrome designs, woven in a similar way, that preclude additional decoration (plate 90). Many of the Addis lengths are for men's ankle-length gowns or waist-length, high-collared jackets. Some have repeating patterns scattered regularly across the surface, while others have subdued twill roundels woven at intervals along them. The roundels are so placed that when the material is cut and sewn to shape, the design is evenly spaced and sits well on the back and front of the finished garment. Woven into the ends of some of the roundel silks are six smaller roundels, grouped in pairs of three, seen on the deep plum-coloured silk. These would have been cut out and tailored into horsehoof-shaped cuffs that covered the backs of the hands. The male elite during the Qing dynasty wore this style of cuff. Although some Chinese still wore roundel-patterned gowns during the Republican era (1911–49), this shape of cuff gradually disappeared because of its

89 Dress length of silk damask 1900–1920 792.5 x 100.3 cm V&A: T.276-1962

90 Silk dress lengths
*c.*1880–1940
Green, V&A: FE. 109-1983
800 x 75.5 cm
Gold/brown
V&A: FE.111A-1983
278 x 79.5 cm
Plum,V&A: FE.112-1983
94 x 78.5 cm
Red, V&A: FE.102-1983
354 x 79.2 cm
Addis Bequest

association with the deposed Manchu Qing ruling clan.

By the mid-1940s, near the end of the Republican period, high demand for gown silk of any sort decreased, although this quality and type of dress material was still favoured in Mongolia and the Himalayan countries, where it was made up into indigenous garments and used in conjunction with local textiles.[5]

An ingenious solution to easy tailoring is provided by a group of pre-patterned velvet lengths, also from the beginning of the twentieth century (V&A T.278 and T.279-1910, FE.105 and FE.106-1983).[6] The contrast between cut and uncut pile on the green

length, and cut pile against a satin ground on the dark indigo length (plate 91), makes for different tonal registers. The cut pile, in the form of little tufts of silk, creates the designs on what would become the main body of both garments, and these tufts also outline collars, edgings, pocket sections and, on some pieces, a spectacle case. These velvet lengths can be patterns for waistcoats or waist-length jackets with sleeves. The tailor, or perhaps home dressmaker, cut around the pattern pieces and joined them together. Care would definitely be needed for this operation because once cut, velvet quickly frays and needs to be expertly faced and lined. We know that short velvet jackets with and without sleeves were very much in vogue in the first half of the twentieth century and that they were mostly, though not exclusively, worn by men over long gowns.

It may seem surprising that long gowns for men persisted in China at a time when the

91 Pre-patterned velvet dress lengths 1900–1920 Dark indigo, V&A: FE.105-1983 424 x 61.5 cm Green, V&A: FE.106-1983 350 x 67 cm Addis Bequest A tag on the green velvet length reads 'No.124 *cha wen rong kan liao 1 jian*' (One length of tea-coloured velvet waistcoat material).

country was attempting to forge itself into a modern nation. The story of dress in twentieth-century China is a complex one, embedded in patriotic and anti-western sentiment, both burning issues of the day. Men who wore gowns during this period were not necessarily old-fashioned but taking pride in being Chinese and attempting to mark themselves off from the West by rejecting the suit with collar and tie. Moreover it was not only the style of their garments but also the materials from which they were made that was important. Suits were tailored from wool, an imported cloth. Silk for gowns was a native product and wearing such clothes was a gesture of support for the home industry. Locally produced cotton imitations of wool cloth began to appear and the different weights were given such names as 'Liberty cloth', 'Patriotic cloth' and 'Sun Yat-sen cloth'.[7]

Despite the seeming traditional nature of men's gowns, the twentieth-century versions differed from their predecessors in several respects. In connection with the material itself, monochrome roundel patterns persisted, as we have seen, but because they may have been linked in people's minds with the dragon configurations of imperial times, one strand of silk design moved away from them to abstract or lattice repeating motifs that were more in keeping with a contemporary vision. The men's clothes in silvery-grey and black (plate 92) give us a good idea of the subdued elegance favoured by Chinese sophisticates of the 1930s and 40s.

Women as well as men adapted their clothing to suit the political, cultural and social changes that swept through Chinese cities from the late nineteenth century.[8] Old shapes and styles persisted but new ones were developed and added to the dress repertoire. As some women cut their hair and no longer bound their feet, so clothes changed to accommodate a changed way of life. One of the adaptations they made to traditional dress was to shorten it and tailor it more sharply so that it outlined the contours of the body, allowing freer movement. Neat jackets, worn thigh-length with matching trousers (plate 93), appeared in the second decade of the twentieth century. A slightly waisted jacket with an above-ankle skirt was prevalent in the 1920s (plate 94), while towards the end of the decade the dress style known as the *qipao* or *cheongsam* (plates 95–98), was taken up by many women, especially those living in urban areas.

All these garment types utilized the material in a different way and an array of patterned fabrics that had not been available before began to appear. There were echoes

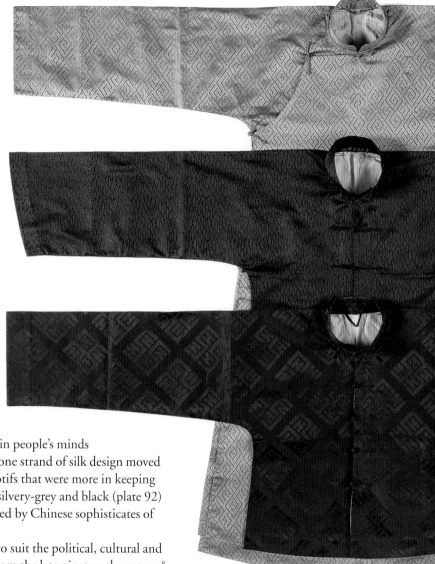

92 Silk robe and jackets for men
1920–40
Grey, V&A: FE.29-1995
127 x 158.5 cm
Black, V&A: FE.25-1995
53.5 x 161 cm
Black, V&A: FE.24-1995
54 x 163 cm
Garrett Collection, purchased with a grant from the Friends of the V&A

of old styles, of course, but the greater mechanization of the silk and cotton industries played its part in transforming how women looked. The new styles of dress displayed the reinvented high neck that was to become a mark of Chinese clothes the world over, and this collar was fashioned out of the same material as the jacket itself, a departure from the edged necklines of imperial times. While some of the new styles retained applied trimmings that, like the collars, became a defining feature, they now had a very different effect. These trimmings were much narrower and no longer encroached on the garment's surface, as was the case on the looser-fitting, wide-sleeved robes and jackets of an earlier period. The newer trend was for the fabric itself, rather than the trims, to be paramount.

From the beginning of the twentieth century, cinema going played a big part in the lives of urban women in Shanghai. By the 1930s, if not before, the clothes of film stars, both Chinese and foreign, influenced what women wore. At the same time, women were exposed to the burgeoning mass print culture of fashion and film magazines, and shopping opportunities increased with the development of specialist stores. Although women would still visit tailors, the first shop specializing in women's apparel in Shanghai was the Hongxiang Fashion Store, founded in 1917; in the same city in 1927, Tang Yinghui, a film star herself, opened the Yunshang Fashion Company.[9]

The new feminine presence came to be exemplified by the *qipao*, a dress style that was developing during the late 1920s and survived outside China, after the 1949 communist take-over, among overseas Chinese, in Hong Kong, and also in Taiwan, where Chiang Kai-shek (1888–1975) set up an opposing government after being defeated by Mao Zedong (1893–1976).

The V&A's collection includes *qipao* made in the Chinese cultural sphere (plates 95–98). The style is also called *cheongsam* in Cantonese, and this term has come to be the more widely used one in English, although spelled in several different ways. Whatever its exact origins, the *qipao* was regularly worn in the 1930s. To some, it seemed a risqué garment because it exposed female flesh and accentuated the curves of the body. It is often associated with the high life of Shanghai, where it took on a glamorous aspect, with entertainers wearing shimmering satin versions. The style was popularized by the advertising industry, and

93 Silk suits for women
Black silk damask,
V&A: FE.56-1995
*c.*1925–35
Jacket 69 x 111.5 cm
Grey silk gauze,
V&A: FE.53-1995
*c.*1915
Jacket 84 x 136.5 cm
Garrett Collection, purchased
with a grant from the Friends
of the V&A

94 Patterned silk jackets
for women
*c.*1925–35
Pink, V&A: FE.62-1995
56 x 110.5 cm
Turquoise, V&A: FE.63-1995
59.5 x 115 cm
Garrett Collection, purchased
with a grant from the Friends
of the V&A

calendar posters distributed by business firms at the New Year used images of women in *qipao* to advertize all manner of products.[10] Not only the *qipao* itself, but also the pose taken up by some of the women in these posters, made them controversial at the time. Today these posters are viewed with nostalgia and much reproduced.[11]

The defining features of the *qipao* are a fitted silhouette, a high collar and side skirt slits. In its classic form, there is a front flap overlapping to the right, which fastens along the collarbone, under the arm and down the right side. The details are subject to changing fashions within the limits of the basic form. It can be sleeveless or have sleeves of any length. The hemline varies, but usually reaches somewhere between the knees and the ankle. The *qipao* can be made of almost any fabric. This represents another departure from tradition for, although it is mostly associated with silk, the *qipao* is found in a range of fibres – cotton, linen, wool, synthetic – making it a highly adaptable style. The material can have a printed or woven repeat pattern across its surface, as in the 1940s examples (plates 95 and 99). If the material is plain, like the 1960s dresses (plate 97), the borders can be patterned. Another popular way of tailoring the style is for the front panel to be pre-embroidered with a sweeping, asymmetric floral or dragon design, leaving the back of the garment unadorned (plate 98). The entire dress is often edged in one or more strips of narrow binding, which is sometimes in plain-coloured bias-cut satin, or else of lace or patterned ribbon. Knot buttons and loops made from fabric are popular. These can be extravagantly shaped and are specially made to suit the pattern or colour of the chosen dress material. In the detail in plate 96, the red and white knot fastenings echo the shape of the bulging-eyed fish on the dress material itself.[12]

A *qipao* has to fit perfectly so it should be custom-made rather than purchased off the peg. The relationship between the customer and her tailor is all-important, as the transaction involves fitting sessions and a negotiated agreement as to material, colourways, trimmings and type of fastenings. These factors, rather than the shape and cut of the dress, are paramount in ensuring a unique garment, one that stands out from its neighbours yet is totally appropriate for the occasion for which it is made.

In the twentieth century, there is no doubt that the *qipao* provided a cross-section of Chinese women with a flattering style of dress that suited their increasingly public lives. Like men's clothes, however, the style became enmeshed in politics. For some, certain traits of the *qipao* were perceived as western and therefore tainted, especially when worn with high-heeled shoes and bobbed hair. In addition to this, with such a wide variety of different materials available, it was almost impossible to tell whether the fabric itself was Chinese-made or imported from overseas. For many, however, the *qipao* seemed both

95 *Qipao* (*cheongsam*) for women, Hong Kong
1940–50
Black silk, V&A: FE.41-1995
104 x 45 cm
Red silk, V&A: FE.42-1995
118 x 45 cm
Garrett Collection, purchased with a grant from the Friends of the V&A

96 *Qipao* (detail of plate 95)
Collar and side-fastening of dress

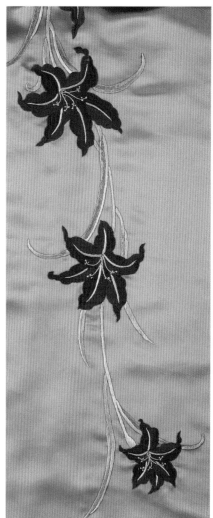

97 *Qipao* (*cheongsam*) for
women, Hong Kong or
San Francisco
1960–70
Grey satin, V&A: FE.52-1997
115 x 51 cm
Turquoise silk and wool
mixture, V&A: FE.57-1997
103 x 52 cm
Given by Richard A. and
Janey M.Y. Cheu
In memory of
Dr Henry D. Cheu

98 *Qipao* (detail of plate 97)
Embroidered front panel

99 Two women in patterned *qipao*, Hong Kong, 1948
Theophilus Peters, a British diplomat, photographed these unnamed ladies during one of his tours of duty in Asia. They were visiting their Chinese homeland, as well as Hong Kong, from Ipoh in today's Malaysia.

modern and Chinese, and it has been suggested that Song Qingling (1892–1981) and Song Meiling (1897–2003), high-profile sisters each married to successive Chinese presidents, did much to endorse and popularize the style.[13]

The survival into the era of industrial manufacturing of a huge spread of different textile designs combined with high technical standards of production is exemplified by a series of offcuts from bolts of material purchased in the 1960s in Hong Kong by an American art historian (plate 100). The precision and high finish of industrial weaving was put to good effect on these silk fabrics, some bearing designs related to Qing prototypes and some of a more innovative nature, but both aimed equally at a global luxury market. The names of the weaving companies woven into the selvages attest to the ongoing practice of identifying the name of the manufacturer for customers in a highly competitive market place. These textiles were woven to be made into clothes, although the range of garment types for which they were destined, from the neo-traditional *qipao* to western eveningwear, was of an unprecedented variety and richness. Bright silks like these were eminently acceptable gifts from travellers returning from Hong Kong and China, their price advantage over Italian printed silk, for example, making them unmissable bargains.

With the death of Chairman Mao in 1976, all kinds of dress regimes became possible in greater China, and the *qipao* was just one of several styles that was revived by Chinese fashion designers. Hong Kong's return to the People's Republic of China in 1997 again heightened the profile of the dress and some saw it as a patriotic garment, a role it had fulfilled in the 1930s and 40s. David Tang, a Hong Kong entrepreneur, sought to

100 Lengths of patterned silk
1960–65
Red, V&A: FE.53-1999
49 x 76 cm
Pink, V&A: FE.55-1999
47.5 x 76 cm
Turquoise, V&A: FE.54-1999
45.5 x 76 cm
White and pink,
V&A: FE.56-1999
26 x 76 cm
Given by Ellen Johnston Laing

101 Trouser suit for a woman
Silk chiffon, Shanghai Tang
(detail of top)
1999
Length of top 51.5 cm
V&A: FE.61-1999
Given by David Tang

develop China's first global brand name, and one of
the high-fashion garments that typified his
Shanghai Tang label was the *qipao*. Customers
visiting his flagship shop, opened in 1994, in Hong
Kong's Pedder Street are able to select from a
colourful range of traditional and modern
reworkings of the style. They can also choose to
have clothes custom-made and are presented with
an abundance of bolts of silk specially woven,
printed and dyed for Shanghai Tang in the People's
Republic. Contemporary garment shapes are also
marketed, although these too retain a Chinese
flavour.

An example from the 1999 collection, a detail
of which is illustrated in plate 101, is a summer
outfit for a woman consisting of a pair of wide
trousers with a matching sleeveless top. The printed
design on the silk chiffon, playing on the 'good
luck' appeal of old-fashioned motifs, and the knot
and loop closure are based on traditional forms.
The ensemble exemplifies the importance of colour
as a signature marker of the Shanghai Tang range.
The products are labelled in English 'Made by
Chinese' as a way of dispelling lingering doubts
about the quality of goods made in greater China.

Vivienne Tam, a Canton-born and Hong Kong-
educated Chinese fashion designer working in New
York also introduced distinctively Chinese imagery
into her designs from the 1990s. The V&A
acquired several pieces from Tam's Mao Collection
of spring 1995. Pictures of Mao Zedong were
ubiquitous during his lifetime and they persisted
after his death in 1976. Some were worked anew
and used in contexts that were sometimes
controversial and contradictory. Vivienne Tam
collaborated with Zhang Hongtu, an artist who
first depicted Mao in his paintings in 1987. She
emblazoned the Chairman's features onto coloured
T-shirts and dresses. The suit and full-length coat
shown here (plates 102 and 103) give a new twist to
the jacquard pictures of Mao that were woven in
such huge quantities in the People's Republic
during the middle decades of the twentieth century
(pages 74 and 75).

The designer herself says that these bi-coloured pieces symbolize the positive and negative effects of Mao's regime, and she recalls her first encounter with the People's Republic of China in the late 1970s and 80s as very different from the one she was used to in Hong Kong. On these particular Tam clothes, the Mao image itself has not been much altered; as a consequence, its use on women's high-fashion garments makes a brazen juxtaposition. The repeating design on heavyweight polyester was printed in Hong Kong. The designer recalls the difficulty of finding a factory to carry out the work and the secrecy with which the finished product was delivered to her.[14] The perceived controversy surrounding its manufacture perhaps served to heighten the collection's appeal and there is no doubt that the fabric, rather than the tailoring, is the paramount feature of these two outfits.

102 Coat and suit for a woman
Polyester, Vivienne Tam
1995
Coat, V&A: FE.43-1998
130 cm
Suit, V&A: FE.45-1998
Jacket 63 cm; skirt 41 cm
Given by Vivienne Tam

103 Suit (detail of plate 102)
Front of skirt
V&A: FE.45-1998

Despite its emphasis on clothing of the rich and middle class, the V&A does also have Chinese dress material from other areas of life. In addition to the high-quality silks manufactured for elite customers that have been discussed, the collection includes precious examples of silk and other fabrics manufactured for less wealthy consumers, although they may well have been relatively valuable and treasured possessions for their original owners.

Just as the People's Republic was opening up to tourists in the 1980s and accelerating a revival of interest in country cottons, so the New Territories, the rural hinterland of the then British colony of Hong Kong, was striving to modernize. A Hong Kong resident and collector, the writer Valery Garrett, perceptively gathered together a sizeable collection of traditional south Chinese clothing that preserved some of the old styles, techniques and fabrics that were then fast disappearing. One such fabric is hemp (*Cannabis sativa*), the weaving of which is every bit as skilful as the weaving of silk regardless of the income levels of the final owners. This dexterity is well exemplified by the hand-woven jacket, believed to date from 1915, shown in plate 104. It is well tailored, all the bindings and button loops being made from bias-cut hemp fabric strips. Before the cultivation of cotton in China, the hemp plant was widely used to make fibres for dress material. It was cultivated in the New Territories of Hong Kong into the twentieth century, which is where the jacket pictured here came from. Today hemp cultivation and processing survives in very limited pockets of production.[15]

Another type of dress fabric that is preserved in the V&A from the Garrett Collection is 'mud silk', sometimes called 'gummed silk' (plate 104). It has a black, glazed appearance on the front, and is a matt, bright orange-brown on the reverse. This type of

104 Jackets from south China and Hong Kong
Hemp, V&A: FE.86-1995
*c.*1915
94 x 112 cm
This jacket was used by the Hakka people, a group that originally migrated to south China from provinces further north.
'Mud' or 'gummed' silk
V&A: FE.78-1995
*c.*1920–50
71 x 175.5 cm
Calendered or coated cotton
V&A: FE.89-1995
*c.*1935–50
71 x 131 cm
This jacket was used by so-called 'boat people' who lived permanently on the water in houseboats.
Garrett Collection, purchased with a grant from the Friends of the V&A

105 Bolt of blue cotton,
in original wrapper
*c.*1980
W. 37 cm
V&A: FE.263-1995
Garrett Collection, purchased
with a grant from the Friends
of the V&A

cloth is waterproof and was used a lot in the 1920s and 30s for making garments, although it is uncertain when the V&A's jacket was made. The silk was coated with vegetable juice and rubbed with mud on one side before being left to dry in the sun.[16]

David Tang, among others, has been instrumental in sustaining the production of this distinctive fabric and has employed it in garment making for his Shanghai Tang label.

Other methods of treating cloth after it has been dyed are sizing and calendering. Both these processes are carried out on cotton, a fabric widely used for dressmaking in China. Besides strengthening the cotton and giving it a water-repellent quality, both techniques enhance the look of the fabric by imparting a shine to the surface. Several different methods of sizing and calendering have been recorded. As people turn to wearing other types of clothes, these post-loom textile treatments are declining skills among the majority of the population of China.[17]

An unopened bolt of strong, blue machine-made cotton from around 1980 (plate 105) provides an idea of how cloth for garments was marketed at that time. It was produced in the People's Republic but sold in Hong Kong, then still a British colony. The blue paper label secured around the cotton states that it was manufactured by the Shanghai Municipal Branch of the China Textiles Import-Export Corporation. The sunflower logo is a commonly occurring device of communist China; the brand name below this reads 'Mallow Flower'. The width of material in this bolt is the same as that used to tailor a traditional *sam* or *shan,* the once-ubiquitous Chinese jacket worn by south Chinese working people (plate 104).[18] It was paired with loose trousers, and worn by both women and men. Women retained the side flap fastening while men favoured a front fastening. Whether the *sam* was made at home or by a tailor, families of modest means had to make the best use of the cloth. Ready-measured cotton bolts such as this guaranteed a minimum of wastage.

Although cotton was grown on China's borderland in Central Asia from an early date, it was in the twelfth century that it really became established in the Lower Yangtze valley. Four centuries later, by the late Ming period, it was cultivated throughout China and a sizeable proportion of the population wore cotton clothes. Cotton technology was a much less complex affair than that required to produce silk; using a simple loom an entire bolt of cotton could be woven in a day. Because of its rather more humble status as an everyday fabric a lot of it remained undecorated, as we have seen.

Cotton was originally dyed with vegetable indigo, synthetic indigo being introduced from the late nineteenth century, although this did not entirely oust the natural dye. The different indigo dye recipes and methods result in a spectrum of blue tones, from the almost black through to lighter hues. This colour range remains associated with rural China, firstly through the many representations of Mao's peasants in the 1950s and 60s, and secondly, in more recent years, through the increased accessibility of China's isolated regions. In these areas, ethnic minority peoples have been encouraged to continue practising their prowess at decorating textiles as well as to wear their distinctive dress.[19] Indigo and cotton are the basis for their highly appealing products, in these cases expertly decorated with stitched and wax resist-dyed patterns.

Not many of the minority peoples' textiles have been collected by the V&A, although

SOME OF THE JUNIORS, BOYS' BLIND SCHOOL, FOOCHOW.

decorated blue cotton textiles of the Han majority, less extensively studied but as technically adept and aesthetically pleasing, do figure in the museum's collection. An indigo wedding quilt from Fujian province has already been discussed (pages 64 and 65), and clothing too, especially that for children, was sometimes patterned with stencil designs in white against a blue ground (plate 106). These blue and white cottons have their origins in rural areas away from the urban mainstream.

Resist-dyed textiles like those shown here (plate 107) come from several areas. The length of unused cotton and the woman's jacket show two different qualities of blue possible with indigo, although wear, exposure to light and perhaps washing have helped to lighten the jacket, which dates from the first half of the twentieth century and is older than the length. The latter is part of the bequest of the diplomat Sir John Addis (1914–83). When Sir John was on his last diplomatic tour of duty in the People's Republic of China in the 1970s, the appeal of this type of textile was once more just beginning to be realized and exploited. His pieces were perhaps made specially for sale in Beijing at that time.[20] Paradoxically, these rural textiles are both rarer and perhaps, to the modern eye, more attractive than some of the luxurious yardage that is better represented in less eclectic collections.

106 Blind boys in a mission school wearing resist-dyed cotton clothing, 1920–35 This photograph is taken from a postcard of a school in Fuzhou, issued by the Church Missionary Society.

107 Dress length and jacket Cotton with resist-dyed decoration Jacket for a woman V&A: T.233-1966 1900–1950 90 x 150 cm Dress length V&A: FE.97-1982 c.1954–74 147 x 44 cm Addis Bequest

6

'IS IT ALL DONE BY HAND?' – CHINESE TEXTILES AND PRODUCTION

Visitors to the Victoria and Albert Museum frequently ask whether the Chinese textiles are handmade. This chapter attempts to answer this question, and to document at least some of the processes of design and production that led to the manufacture of the textiles discussed in this book.

While it is the case that all of the embroidery was certainly 'done by hand', this needs to be qualified with reference to textiles patterned on the loom, which are discussed later (page 104). Even as regards embroidery, because most of the Chinese textiles in the V&A span the period of China's growth as an industrial nation in the late nineteenth and twentieth centuries, the thread used for the hand stitching might have been machine reeled, while the background materials for the embroidered designs may have been made on power looms either within China or elsewhere.

Colourful skeins from 1930s China (plate 108) provide an idea of what some of the 'raw material' for the embroidery process looked like. They are packaged in folded paper stamped in red with the name of a Canton firm, the Hua Xing Company, which welcomes customers to buy its different lines of multi-coloured embroidery thread. The luminous skeins are of flat silk strands with hardly any twist. Originally, each package consisted of a full range of tonal gradations of a particular colour, from light to dark, although today the contents of the packets are mixed up. This type of thread would have been used to create the shiny straight stitches in shaded tones that are typical of Chinese embroidery of the nineteenth and twentieth centuries. While this thread is liable to become wispy, a dextrous embroiderer manipulates it so as to preserve its smooth silkiness.

Silk, the unravelled thread from a moth's cocoon, is a strong, continuous filament. Unlike wool and cotton, which only ever consist of short fibres, it does not need to be spun to form a workable yarn. Silk is, however, given various degrees of twist in a process known as throwing, and twisted yarn gives a different effect when used as embroidery thread as it is less reflective. While not all thread and stitch variations used in Chinese embroidery are represented by the pieces in this book, there is nonetheless a profusion of techniques that give us an idea of the ingenuity of the makers.

Embroidery stitches can be categorized in several different ways. Sometimes the groupings are named after the motif that they are most commonly used for. Such examples in Chinese embroidery might be *ba songmi*, or 'forming pine needles', and *qiang lin*, or 'forming scales'. Other stitch categories rely on the method of manipulating needle and

108 Silk skeins for embroidery
1930–40
18 cm
V&A: FE.202: 6-1968

109 Embroidered silk
birthday hanging (detail)
1880–1920
123.2 x 48.9 cm
V&A: T.176-1961
Given by Miss Catherine
O'Brien-Butler

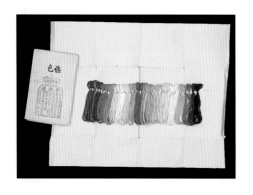

thread and therefore, to some extent, on the appearance of the finished work. So, in China, the most commonly found stitches can be divided into *ping zhen*, meaning 'flat stitch' and translated into English as 'satin stitch', *dazi zhen,* literally meaning 'making seeds stitch' and known in English as 'knot stitch', *ding zhen*, meaning 'fastening stitch' and best translated as 'couching', and *zhi zhen*, 'line stitch', called 'straight stitch' in English. Other kinds of stitches are used but most of them are combinations and variations of these basic types. Chain stitch (*suo xiu*) and a technique sometimes used in combination with chain stitch, known as needle-looping (*huanzhen xiu*), are forms of decorative stitching that were used on Chinese embroideries in earlier centuries but are not represented on many of the V&A's textiles.[1]

A detail (plate 109) from the set of panels on pages 56 to 58 reveals how creatively the stitching has been deployed to obtain different visual effects particularly appropriate to the medium of embroidery. The scene is set in the remote past and depicts one of the twenty-four filial piety stories in which Huang Xiang is seen cooling his father's bed with a fan. The direction in which the stitch is worked, the starting and finishing point of the stitch, the density of stitches and the amount of background material left blank as part of the design, plus the outlining, overlaying or embellishing of blocks of stitching, are all technical factors that determine how the piece will look. Usually, the stitches fill in the outlines of the pattern. Sometimes the stitches are worked according to a geometric grid, using the interlocking threads of the woven ground material as a guide (page 115).[2]

Certain embroideries are assigned to different schools of work because they supposedly manifest particular features. These schools take their names either from the regions where they were made or from the families that first produced the work. Places famous for distinctive embroidery both now and in the past are Suzhou, Guangdong, Sichuan and Hunan, although textiles in the V&A are not on the whole assignable to one school or another. There is no doubt that these different styles existed and some of these schools took on a new lease of life in the twentieth century, moving away from the traditional to develop innovatory designs and techniques.

Alongside this development, the craft was widely practised for profit in professionally organized workshops. Such business ventures may have found it expedient to 'brand' their products with regional names, thus adding to their appeal.[3] An example of an embroidery style named after a family is that of Gu, whose women practitioners originally lived in the Shanghai mansion called the Dew Fragrance Garden, famous in the sixteenth and seventeenth centuries for the artistic production of embroidery pictures after famous paintings.[4] Again, while vestiges of this style might be discernible on some of the pieces in the museum, there are few known products of this famous workshop outside east Asian collections.

The embroidery on all the V&A pieces was undisputedly hand done. We are less sure about the conditions surrounding the production of individual pieces, for these differed across time and region. By the late Qing dynasty (1644–1911), from which most of the museum's Chinese textiles date, some of the embroideries were created in the domestic sphere by women endeavouring to supplement their household incomes. Even women from the upper stratum of society were expected to work productively, embroidery taking the place of weaving from the Ming period (1368–1644) onwards. Many items, however, were made in commercial workshops, where different artisans, sometimes male and sometimes female, specialized in certain kinds of work.

Laying down gold-wrapped thread as an outline or as an in-filling for scales might be one such specialization. Foil sticking (*tie jin*), sometimes used in conjunction with embroidery (*ying jin*) and sometimes with painting, is another. Dowry items such as the V&A's Straits beaded pieces and the blue and white cross-stitch cottons (pages 66 to 68) continued to be made at home in the first part of the twentieth century on a non-commercial basis, although it is unclear which other marriage textiles in the museum were made in this way and which ones were ordered from shops specializing in wedding artefacts. Decorative textiles that were made for export or sold within China to travellers and sojourners from overseas were made by outworkers at home or in commercial ateliers.[5]

Techniques new to the Chinese repertoire grew up specially to satisfy this foreign demand, an example being drawn thread work and white work, with the two often being combined in one product (plate 110). Ramie, from a woody plant (*Boehmeria nivea*) of

110 Ramie curtain
(detail of plate 35)
Drawn thread work edging
V&A: FE.150-1983

111 Advertisement for Swatow work, Hong Kong, 1958 The Swatow Weng Lee Co. was established in China in 1917 and continued to trade through Hong Kong after the founding of the People's Republic in 1949.

the nettle family, proved an ideal fabric for this and its production for export items increased in China at the beginning of the twentieth century.[6]

Drawn thread work is created by first removing, or drawing out, certain threads in the ground fabric and then using them to group and sew together the threads that remain. Although the V&A curtains came into the museum with an early nineteenth-century date from the donor, according to a United States Commercial Report the drawn thread industry was given a boost by Christian missionaries who introduced it into Shantou (Swatow) in the 1880s, and by 1921 it engaged 10,000 workers. The same report gives the starting date of white work, that is white embroidery on a cream or white ground, as around 1900. For both kinds of work, a local contractor supplied the materials to the workers and then collected and paid for the finished articles.

In another recorded case in Chaozhou, a prefecture near Shantou that was originally a centre for the production of dragon robes and theatre costumes, the designing was carried out by men in studios dedicated to this work before the material was distributed to homeworkers.[7] The term 'Swatow work' quickly became synonymous with small embroidered souvenirs (plate 111) of several kinds and continues to be marketed under that name.

Little is known about how the drawn thread and white work designs, or any others, were delineated onto the cloth, but surviving pattern books show the repertoire of motifs available to the embroiderer.[8] These were chosen and ordered as the occasion demanded. As in the case of stitching techniques, motifs were combined and recombined to create variety, rather than something novel, within a familiar design framework. The way the embroiderer 'coloured in' identical motifs was crucial to particularizing each piece. Templates, pouncing and freehand painting may all have been used as a guide for the embroidery, the details of which were left to the needleworker. There are only a few clues

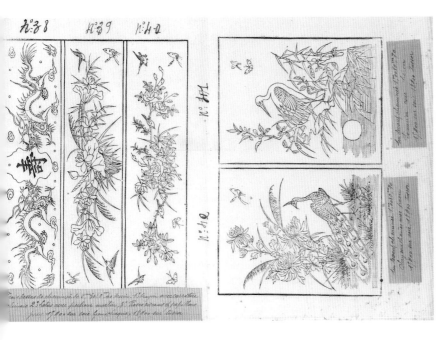

112 Page from embroidery
pattern book, Nam-Quat of
Tonkin (Vietnam)
1915–20
42 x 76 cm
V&A: FE.104-1997
Given by John Lust

113 Painted silk
(detail of plate 33)
V&A: T.3-1948

to this aspect of Chinese embroidery on pieces in the collection and these are in the form
of occasional remains of black ink outlines or coded instructions (page 73).

A large-format printed pattern book (plate 112) does not seem to be primarily for the
use of the artisans carrying out the work, but for customers to choose and order a
product. Dating from the mid teens or twenties of the twentieth century, its many
different designs, sometimes one to a page and sometimes more, show a range of plants,
birds, butterflies and beasts. Entire layouts are given, as well as single elements. It was
used by the firm of Nam-Quat in Vietnam, which was at the time a colonial possession of
France. The title page is therefore in French, as are the hand-written descriptions with
prices. A large number of ethnic Chinese have settled in Vietnam over the centuries and
may have provided the business impetus behind this embroidery enterprise, which was
undoubtedly aimed at least in part at expatriate Europeans. To meet the high demand for
such decorated items, the firm had branches elsewhere, including Shanghai, and its desire
to reach an international clientele is evident from its entry and medal success in
competition. It had the ability to produce many kinds of interior furnishings in a variety
of colourways. The four designs shown here are for fire screens.

There are more embroidered Chinese textiles in the museum than any other kind and
in this respect the collection reflects China's output at the end of the nineteenth century.
During that period, embroidery was the most common technique employed to decorate
silk and cotton, although as mentioned (page 80) its use diminished on clothing as the
twentieth century wore on. Likewise, the collection has relatively large numbers of
painted silks because these were made expressly for export to Europe and the Americas
and were not marketed within China itself. Like the embroideries, they are valued for
their handcrafted artistry and decorative charm, and on close inspection exhibit a
spectrum of competencies from the poorly executed to the highly proficient (plate 113).

Handmade, from whatever period, does not necessarily equate with high quality, and it should be borne in mind that, where China is concerned, factory conditions prevailed across several crafts from early times. This meant an organized workforce, managed by overseers who may not have been producers themselves and who broke down the work process into specialized smaller tasks in order to facilitate speedier production. On the one hand, this kind of structure permits careful quality control, and ateliers can take on an educational role in disseminating knowledge to young workers.[9] But it can also mean that, with faster and therefore greater output, financial gain takes precedence over maintaining standards.

The painted silk industry of south China responded to the demands of the export trade in this way. Although we have no exact information about how the work was divided up, we know the processes involved in producing painted silks. The silk was first prepared by sizing it with alum. The design was then delineated either freehand or by pressing a heavily inked paper drawing onto the surface. Next, a chalk or lead white layer was affixed over the motifs and the colours were then brushed on. Lastly, the motifs were accentuated with a thin silver outline. Today, this has tarnished and is difficult to detect with the naked eye. Different groups of artisans might have carried out these separate tasks.[10]

Resist dyeing seems likely to have been more widespread in China than the few examples in the V&A would lead us to believe. The western appetite for Chinese painted silk in the eighteenth century and Chinese embroideries in the following centuries defined the kinds of textile that form the bulk of the collection. It may have been a contributing factor in the decline of other processes. While indigo resist-dyed textiles from Japan have been treasured and their producers revered due to the campaigning efforts of prominent craft theorists in the early twentieth century, no such high-profile undertaking occurred in China, despite the best efforts of some Chinese folklorists.[11] Production methods were therefore not widely recorded in precise detail, and it is not self-evident from the finished article alone which particular materials and techniques were used.

Because the patterning on these pieces was done by hand, we can say that they were handcrafted, although some of the background material might have been machine-made. However, we know neither what sort of establishment produced these dyed cottons, nor whether more than one artisan carried out the work. Stencils were certainly involved and evidence from the production of papercuts, a craft akin to stencil cutting, might signal that the stencil cutter was a specialized craftsperson who was not involved in the application of paste and dye. Literature regarding this type of cloth describes the stencils as cut from oiled paper, and the paste used to resist the dye as made from lime and bean flour. The dye does not colour those parts of the material that are covered with the thick, set paste and when this is scraped off, the pattern is revealed in blue and white. The stencil can be moved along the cloth and used again because it is given a wax or persimmon juice coating to strengthen it and make it waterproof.[12] Where several colours besides blue are used – and this is more unusual – the additional dye is brushed on.

When the V&A acquired the coloured cotton wedding quilt (plate 114), an informative printed text fortuitously came with it relating the stages of its production. In this case, the stencils provided the outlines of the picture, which were delineated onto the hand-woven cotton with a paste of three kinds of rice, alum, glue and soot. The red,

114 Cover for a quilt, cotton with resist-dyed decoration (detail of plate 70)
V&A: FE.19-1984
This detail shows a squirrel on a trailing pumpkin vine, a motif that sends wishes for many sons to continue the family lineage.

green and yellow areas were painted on by hand, the paint being a mixture of dye, green persimmons, egg white and bean curd. These coloured portions were next protected with the resist-paste and the whole cloth immersed in the indigo dye solution. Once the paste was removed with boiling water, the fine details, such as facial features, were added with a brush. The accompanying text also states that 'forty days of sunshine' were required to satisfactorily complete the process.

Wax- and stitch-resist techniques, favoured by people living in south-west China, flourish more widely today than the paste and stencil process. Other dye patterning methods – tie-dyeing, block printing and clamp-resist dyeing (*jia xie*) – dwindled, although the museum has surviving examples of the latter on some Tang dynasty (AD 618–906) Buddhist silk banner fragments from the Mogao Grottoes on the Silk Road, near Dunhuang in north-west China and, for a later period, the thin silk coverings used to protect Tibetan *thangkas* are also decorated this way.[13]

115 Painted design
for a textile label
1895–1915
19 x 23 cm
V&A: FE.498-1992
Given by Dr Margaret Bennett

It may seem strange that the country that invented printing from carved woodblocks in the Tang period did not seem to exploit the technique fully when it came to textile decoration. It had to wait until modern times and the introduction of industrial roller, flatbed and rotary screen printing to speedily cover yards of cotton and silk with dyed repeat patterns after they had been woven.

Tensions between objects constructed as handmade and those seen as industrial products, and hence part of a wider world of industrial design, have been a consistent part of the way in which Chinese textile products have been perceived in the West since at least the nineteenth century. The V&A has been a particular site in which those still unresolved contests have been played out. To this day, they remain active within the museum in debates over the types of acquisition, collecting and display in which it engages. The colourful cotton bolts from the late 1970s (page 46) are typical examples. From this period on, China experienced an economic boom, as the politics of the Maoist years receded (1949–76).

A diversity of textile types is now produced there. The current impact of globalization on the textile industry in China is to a great extent a factor of the presence there of a large, competent workforce, the labour costs of which remain relatively low in international terms. To an extent, this recapitulates the process at the end of the Qing period, in the late nineteenth and early twentieth centuries, when foreign firms were first able to set up operations in China.[14]

One testimony to this early phase of the incorporation of Chinese textile production into global markets lies in the museum's collection of textile label designs. Bales of cloth exported from China to Britain bore a pictorial trademark depicting scenes from Chinese life or mythology. These brightly coloured labels (plate 115) were printed on paper from original paintings. The painted designs had to be approved either by a company agent in Shanghai or by the importer's offices in Britain to ensure that they had not been used before, and for this purpose a file record of each trademark was retained. The label proofs in the V&A are connected with the firms of Thorne and Co.

Ltd. of Finsbury Square, London, which ceased trading in 1935, and of Norbury, Natzio and Co. Ltd. of Old Trafford, Manchester. Some of the designs are dated, and the years range from 1895 to 1915.

It should be noted in this respect that China also imported cotton yarn and cotton piece goods from the West during this period.[15] The museum has little information about either the imported or exported textile products themselves. It seems likely that they were patterned cottons, perhaps printed or woven with simple stripes and checks, a class of textiles mostly overlooked by western museums as too every day to merit inclusion in their collections.

Embroidery and painting, resist dyeing and printing, plus the finishes discussed on pages 91 to 93, are all post-loom processes, that is, the decoration and effects were added *after* the material was woven. Some of the Chinese textiles in the V&A were decorated *as part of* the weaving process. They came off the loom with a ready-finished pattern across the surface. The purpose of a loom is to hold a closely spaced set of parallel threads under tension (warp threads), so that other threads (weft threads) can be passed in and out of them at right angles.

116 Robe of tapestry woven silk (detail of plate 85)
V&A: FE.41-1988

One weaving technique from China that has arguably engaged the attention of museums more than others is silk tapestry (*kesi,* or *k'o-ssu* as seen in the romanization in older books), a loom-patterning operation in which the weaving process is done completely by hand.[16] It relies on the experience and ingenuity of the craftworker, who sits at a simple loom plying individual colours in and out of the taut, undyed longitudinal warp threads. The design is laid beneath these stretched threads, or else actually painted onto them, both the cartoon and the warp threads gradually disappearing as the weaver works across the cloth, using as many different shuttles as there are colours in the pattern. The small shuttles on which the patterning threads are wound do not pass right across the width of the cloth but are worked in and out only in limited areas.

A work in progress on a tapestry loom therefore has several shuttles resting at intervals across its surface. The completed section of the textile, nearest to the weaver, does not grow at a uniform rate, as in other weaving methods, because one colour area is at least partly finished before the surrounding colours are filled in around it. This method of working can be discerned on the peony bud at the top of the detailed picture of the robe with deer roundels (plate 116). The light blue silk that forms the calyx above the leaf was shuttled to and fro in an undulating line, and then the red shuttle was taken up to fill in the spaces and create the closed peony petals.

Although the binding system – the order of interlacing the horizontal and vertical threads – is a simple one in the case of tapestry weaving, as in the case of embroidery, variations on the basic technique and combinations of these are utilized. Therein lies the artistry of such pictorial pieces. The way the weaver manipulates the shuttles at the point where one colour ends and the next begins, outlines some of the colour areas, incorporates gold thread into the weaving and winds two colours onto one shuttle for a mottled effect are all deft skills employed to interpret and enhance the design.

For other types of woven cloth, the weft threads are inserted into the warps in a predetermined order and, unlike in *kesi,* both the warp and weft may be visible in the final design. Efficient and precise forward planning is necessary and once the loom is set up there is no opportunity to make changes in the patterning. So that the weaver does not have to insert the weft in and out of each warp thread individually, devices for lifting and separating groups of warp threads have been developed. These various devices open up a space, called a shed, which allows the weft to be passed easily from side to side of the material, considerably speeding up the weaving process.

Many of the patterned silks from China were woven on the drawloom.[17] This tall structure required a worker to sit at the top of the loom and batch together the warp threads in various configurations, lifting them to open up a passage for the weaver below to pass the weft from one side to the other. It was exceptionally hard work, preceded by meticulous preparation to mount the many warp threads side by side on the loom. The yellow cushion cover for a shaped chair back (plate 117) may have been woven this way. The very closely packed warp threads of yellow silk interweave with a set of matching yellow weft threads to form a satin foundation weave, but in addition to this the warp threads have a second job to do. They bind in a supplementary set of wefts of different colours that create the dragon and cloud pattern. Other textiles in the collection, patterned on the loom, use a variety of binding systems to achieve their designs.

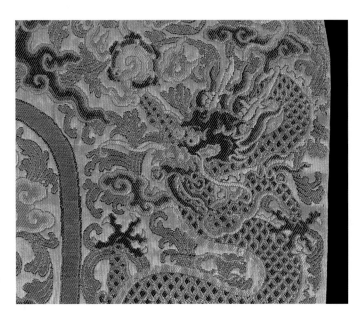

Like some other kinds of Chinese textile production, pattern weaving was broken down into specialisms. Only dexterous artisans could handle the gold threads, sometimes wound foil and sometimes flat strips, and the peacock feather filaments that are woven into several examples. Likewise, the weaving of damasks calls for particular abilities, as do velvets and gauzes, the manufacture of the latter two relying on the manipulation of an extra set of warp threads.[18]

117 Cushion cover pattern woven silk (detail of plate 12) V&A: T.135-1917

Pattern books or swatch samples from the large number of weaving establishments that existed throughout China have not been found. While there must have been some kind of initial design, perhaps a freehand drawing, it seems that a prototype of the weaving was constructed in a coarse yarn without a loom and that this was the only intermediary between the drawing and the finished textile. A foreman might have called out the order of shuttling or the weavers themselves might have sung as a mnemonic to the steps required.[19] The complexities of all types of pattern weaving meant that several expert workers must have understood the entire process, even if they were not adept at carrying out each one. Since the Song dynasty (960–1279), most weavers of richly figured cloth were professional men who learned their trade from a young age. The Ming and Qing imperial workshops manufactured the most elaborate silks and set the technical standards for the private concerns that operated alongside them. Today, we do not always know which kind of enterprise the surviving silks came from. Moreover, although a textile's internal weave structure can be analyzed under magnification, we cannot be sure of the type of loom used for specific pieces.[20]

Throughout the centuries technical innovations both in reeling equipment for the yarn and in loom design resulted in the capacities of the hand being supplemented by various mechanical devices.[21] In 1906, an innovation known as the jacquard attachment reached China. It was named after its inventor, Joseph Marie Jacquard (1752–1834), who perfected a mechanical method of producing realistic patterning and pictures on cloth. From that time on, woven pictures were a regular part of China's textile output. The jacquard replaced the drawboy at the top of the loom with a series of cards, punched according to the dictates of the design. The weaver manipulated these by pressing down on a pedal as well as plying the shuttle.

By itself, this invention did not do away with the need to pass the shuttle from side to side by hand nor to beat down the inserted weft thread to the edge of the already completed fabric. Although the design is programmed by the punched cards, the loom still needs a hand operative. Repeat floral and other designs could be woven this way and we have already seen how the innovation was exploited to produce life-like silk pictures under the Maoist regime (pages 73 to 75). The communist pictures from the 1960s and 70s were made with jacquard mechanisms attached to power looms. These require less strength and skill to operate and the training period is much shorter than for a handloom. The factory worker may oversee several power looms at a time, watching for breakdowns and faults. Harnessing steam, electricity and occasionally water to provide extra levels of power largely replaced hand with automated weaving by the mid-twentieth century.

The introduction of power looms for weaving silk was, however, only undertaken very slowly and lagged behind the mechanization of cotton production. Electric power looms were introduced to Shanghai in 1915 and to Hangzhou in 1921.

A report of a five-year survey of the silk industry of south China, published in 1925, records only four factories in Guangdong province with modern machinery.[22] Moreover, China imported Irish linen yarn, cotton, sewing machines and textile dyes, the latter exemplified by a 1926 poster in the museum's collection (plate 118). The Chinese lady, fashionably dressed and arranging flowers in a modern room, advertises dye stuffs from DuPont, a chemical conglomerate that is again investing in Shanghai in the twenty-first century.

While natural dyes from plant, animal and mineral sources persisted in some, mostly rural, areas synthetic dyes, some more successful than others, penetrated China in the last three decades of the nineteenth century. The accidental discovery by the English teenage chemist William Henry Perkin (1838–1907) of synthetic mauve in 1856 led the way to other developments. These new dyes were better suited to automated commercial textile

118 Calendar Poster for DuPont dye, 1926
76 x 52.5 cm
V&A: FE.479-1992

production than natural dyes because they could provide consistent colouring across large batches of cloth. In the 1920s and 30s, German dyes, some of the most scientifically advanced at the time, were marketed in China and, during the Japanese occupation (1937–45), the mobile tailoring unit of the communist Eighth Route Army sent people into the blockaded port cities to retrieve German khaki dye. This was issued to the soldiers in the pockets of their undyed uniforms for do-it-yourself colouring.[23]

The carpets that were produced in China during the same decades were also

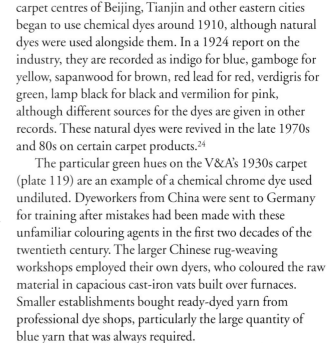

sometimes made from yarn dyed with German dyes. The carpet centres of Beijing, Tianjin and other eastern cities began to use chemical dyes around 1910, although natural dyes were used alongside them. In a 1924 report on the industry, they are recorded as indigo for blue, gamboge for yellow, sapanwood for brown, red lead for red, verdigris for green, lamp black for black and vermilion for pink, although different sources for the dyes are given in other records. These natural dyes were revived in the late 1970s and 80s on certain carpet products.[24]

The particular green hues on the V&A's 1930s carpet (plate 119) are an example of a chemical chrome dye used undiluted. Dyeworkers from China were sent to Germany for training after mistakes had been made with these unfamiliar colouring agents in the first two decades of the twentieth century. The larger Chinese rug-weaving workshops employed their own dyers, who coloured the raw material in capacious cast-iron vats built over furnaces. Smaller establishments bought ready-dyed yarn from professional dye shops, particularly the large quantity of blue yarn that was always required.

Carpets and rugs were handmade on basic upright looms and, as in the case of some other loom products, machine-spun yarns made from cotton for the warp threads and wool for the weft knots were sometimes used. These were not introduced uniformly and so cannot be used as sure pointers

119 Carpet, wool pile (detail of plate 56) V&A: FE.2-2003

to dating. From the first decade of the twentieth century up until 1950, machine-spun cotton for Chinese carpet making was mostly imported. It was called 'overseas 3-ply' (*yang san gu*) and was doubled for strength. Wool came from north-west China.[25]

The carpets discussed in this book were made by creating an individual knot around every two vertical warp threads. A type of figure-of-eight knot was used. Sometimes this is termed 'asymmetrical' and sometimes, in the European trade, it is called 'Persian'. The Chinese name is *kai kou jie*, or 'open knot'. The knotting proceeds in a line across the width of the carpet, with several weavers spread out along a bench working on the same piece. The ends of the knots are cut, leaving tufts on the front. These tightly packed cut ends form the characteristic carpet pile.

In this respect, Chinese carpets are similar to those made in some other parts of the world; it is the design, the colouring, the density of the pile, the method of finishing the edges and the way the details are worked that mark them out as coming from China. Particularly significant in this regard are the rugs first made in the 1920s and 30s, mostly to the order of foreign firms, displaying a range of neo-traditional designs as well as modernist patterns. Some of these, like the V&A's green and cream carpet, are worked in a distinctive technique known as 'closed-back', which makes them especially compact. This involves depressing one warp of each pair so that it is behind its partner rather than lying alongside it. In the 1920s and perhaps earlier, completed Chinese carpets begun to have the outlines of their patterns incised in relief with pointed shears. From that time too, a lustre was chemically imparted to the carpets, a process that happens naturally over the years but which was speeded up by this washing process.[26]

With the rather specific demands of consumers in North America after the First World War (1914–18), there was a need to draw up accurately rendered designs to bridge the distance between the maker and the market. The V&A has a set of such designs (plate 120) that shed light on the working practices of the Chinese carpet industry. They date from the late 1930s and originate from the firm of Liebermann Waelchli and Co. of Tianjin.

We learn of other possible design arrangements from printed catalogues produced for prospective customers. There are picture carpets loosely based on Chinese painting styles, ones with simple borders and a minimal field design in blues and creams, asymmetrical patterns where elements from the border spill over into the field, and the true deco pieces which are borderless with abstracted motifs. Aubusson, Savonneries, Persian and Spanish carpet patterns were copied and adapted. The Chinese Carpets and Rugs Factory, operating out of Shanghai, gave easy instructions for ordering a personalized carpet in its 1921 catalogue. Motifs could be changed around and colours altered to suit individual taste. 'Why have bare floors in the home when fashionable Chinese rugs can be purchased direct from the manufacturer at so reasonable a price?' the catalogue asks.[27] Designs served the dual purpose of providing directions for both manufacturers and consumers.

The Chinese rug-weaving industry today follows the work format of previous decades. First the design is enlarged in black and white to the actual size of the carpet and is either propped up close behind the loom as a guide or transferred onto the stretched warp threads. The weavers refer to a small-scale, filled-in design as a colour guide while they work and, as in the case of embroidery and tapestry, the quality and nuancing of the finished patterning very much depends on the experience and sensitivity of the weaver.

Today many carpet weavers in China are women and it is likely that women wove the Great Leap Forward silk pile rug on page 72. Earlier in the twentieth century, at the height of foreign interest in China's rug industry, child labour was prevalent. The apprentice system in operation at the time is outlined in a report conducted by the Chinese Social and Political Science Association in 1924. Weavers slept and ate in the workrooms, which were always full of choking wool dust, and the dehumanizing conditions of factory employment, whether it involved work carried out by hand or by machinery, were the norm. Exploitation and fragile patterns of employment were not, of course, unique to China – textile production in many cultures has been notoriously harsh and unrewarding.[28]

120 Painted designs for carpets
1935–40
35 x 25.8 cm
Green, V&A: FE.109-2002
Beige, V&A: FE.113-2002
Pink, V&A: FE. 116-2002
Blue, oval, V&A: FE.118-2002
Given by Susan Sackner

DESIGN No. 365.

DESIGN No. 613.

DESIGN No. 114.

DESIGN No. 309.

7 COLLECTORS, DONORS AND DEALERS

I T IS OFTEN BELIEVED THAT great numbers of objects came to the V&A from the 1851 Great Exhibition in London's Hyde Park. While it is true that some certainly did originate there, and in subsequent international exhibitions, they were not transferred wholesale, and Chinese donations were rather few.[1]

The V&A acquired Chinese textiles in several different ways, and it is certainly the case that we know more about their procurement by the museum than we do about their life in China before they came into European hands. People sold, gave and bequeathed textiles to the museum. Some were dealers, others collectors, souvenir hunters, entrepreneurs and scholars, and these roles often merged. Many of those who offered pieces had no specialist knowledge and may have inherited the textiles from family members.

Connections with China were not always thought important enough to register in the museum files. Those that are recorded give us a picture of imperialist enterprise, travellers' tales and, occasionally, missionary endeavour. Most donors were Europeans. Many were in China to fight, trade, negotiate or convert; only in very recent years are donors with Chinese names listed in the museum's acquisition books. This chapter recounts the story of the accumulation of Chinese textiles by the V&A and, by looking closely at a number of examples, reveals the agency of outsiders in setting the agenda of study within the museum.[2]

Two characters closely identified with early museum textile acquisitions, among them Chinese ones, are the Reverend Dr Franz Bock (1823–99) and Dr Robert Forrer (1860–1947). Their relationship with the V&A, while yet to be fully explored, points up the interconnection between dealing, collecting and scholarship, a theme that runs as a constant through any study of the history of museums.

Neither Bock nor Forrer had any specialist expertise in things Chinese, but their knowledge of the textile field in general was formidable. They assembled their collections, each comprising thousands of pieces, and then used them as a resource for scholarship, writing about them and very often publishing them before selling the pieces on to the museum. Bock's association with the museum lasted nearly fifty years, from 1856 to 1898, and silk fragments from China and Central Asia acquired from him in 1860 and given dates between the Yuan dynasty (1260–1368) and the mid-Ming dynasty (1368–1644) are among the very first east Asian loom-patterned textiles to come into the V&A (pages 9 and 21).[3]

Robert Forrer of Strassburg (Strasbourg) first appears in the museum records in 1893, when he offered a collection of European printed linens, a subject on which he had already published. In 1899 the first of Forrer's Chinese pieces entered the collection

121 Fragment of bi-coloured silk damask
1550–1650
43 x 35 cm
V&A: 1404-1899
Forrer Collection

122 Picture of tapestry woven silk, Dragon Boat Festival
1750–1850
79 x 90 cm
V&A: 1647-1900

(plate 121) along with some early European and Persian silks. The example here is a bi-coloured silk patterned with a graceful design of lotus flowers. A likely date for this piece is the late Ming period. Like Bock, Forrer had acquired many of his textiles from shrines and reliquaries in German church treasuries, although in neither case is it clear exactly what form the transactions took. There is no doubt that at least some of the Chinese textiles acquired from these two scholar collectors were of considerable age, and the purchases are symptomatic of the museum's turnaround from issues of contemporary good design to the more disciplined historical and aesthetic concerns of art history. As already mentioned, in the 1920s and 30s the V&A took on several hundred medieval archaeological fragments brought back from Central Asia by Sir Aurel Stein (1862–43), another formidable scholar who also published the pieces before depositing them in several museums (pages 6, 9, 18 and 20).[4]

Throughout its history, the museum has regularly been approached by donors and dealers, some knowledgeable and others not so, with offers of possible acquisitions. In the case of Chinese textiles, rarely do curators seem to have gone looking for pieces. Rather, they have assessed items brought to their attention over the years, but have not always actively sought out specific artefacts. This situation favoured the dealers who were best able to petition curators persuasively as to the value of their pieces.

Herr Kieruff, an entrepreneur who corresponded with the V&A from the Villa Peking, Hellerup, in Denmark, at the turn of the twentieth century, seems not to have been known to the museum at all before he made a single offer of over 400 Chinese textiles. One of those acquired is shown in plate 122. It is from a set of four silk tapestries dating between 1750 and 1850 that depict dragon boats re-enacting a legendary event in Chinese history. They are searching for the drowned body of the loyal minister Qu Yuan, of the fourth to third century BC. The Dragon Boat Festival is held annually to commemorate his heroic suicide. Not all of Kieruff's textiles were retained by the museum and it is unclear how the final choice was made (V&A 1644 to 1663-1900, 1601 to 1647-1901).

It is tempting to speculate that Kieruff, who had amassed his textiles in Beijing, may have known about a V&A commission entrusted to Stephen Bushell (1844–1908), also resident in that city, to augment the museum's collection of Chinese art. As things worked out, Bushell, the first person who knew Chinese to write about the collection at South Kensington, concentrated on acquiring ceramics for the museum, so the Danish dealer could have taken the opportunity to offer textiles.[5] However, there is currently no evidence to support the view that the two Europeans were aware of each other's interests.

By the middle of the twentieth century a more usual route for Chinese textiles to enter the museum was via dealers whose primary interest lay with other Chinese antique artefacts, namely ceramics, jades and bronzes. This pattern of taking on textiles almost as an afterthought is exemplified by the respected London West End galleries of Spink and Son Ltd and Bluett and Sons, both specialists in the field of Chinese art, supplying occasional textiles along with other kinds of objects.

The material on offer at this time by these dealers, although not vastly different either in quality or type from that acquired in the first hundred years of the museum's existence,

123 Wall hanging of tapestry woven silk
1800–1900
117 x 142 cm
V&A: T.140-1956

is suggestive of an increasing expertise on the part of both the dealers themselves and certainly the museum. In 1956 four items were selected by George Wingfield Digby (1911–89) out of a possible twenty offered by Bluett, an indication that the museum and its eminent head of textiles were becoming more selective (V&A T.138 to T.141-1956). One of the pieces is a celebration valance (plate 123). Dating from the nineteenth century, it is woven to shape in the tapestry technique and shows dragons and filial sons. Perhaps part of Wingfield Digby's justification for purchasing at all was the provenance of the collection. Some of the pieces had belonged to Sir Perceval Yetts (1878–1957), who became a towering figure of early Chinese art and archaeology, establishing the subject at London University.[6]

A decade later, the V&A also did business with

Collet's Chinese Bookshop, a very different kind of firm from Spink and Bluett, but again one exclusively devoted to China. This left-wing bookshop in Great Russell Street, opposite the British Museum, was one of several Collet's outlets, the first having opened in 1934.[7] Collet's sold mainly books on Chinese culture, and it was one of the few outlets for publications from the People's Republic in the 1960s and 70s, when political relations between China and the West were under strain. Perhaps because of its socialist credentials, Collet's was also able to import from China various art and craft items, some of which were called 'antique'.

The Cixi scroll on page 59 is one such Collet's purchase, and an incomplete album of embroidered Lohans, pictured here (plate 124), is another. It dates from the time of the revival of embroidery as an art at the beginning of the twentieth century, and is worked in neutral tones to echo brush painting. These Lohans, or perfected persons, are from Buddhist iconography and are sometimes found in a group of sixteen or eighteen. Only nine survive in the V&A album.

When considering acquisitions, the museum is undoubtedly swayed by the details of past ownership. The decision to purchase the Cixi scrolls from Collet's and the Yetts textiles from Bluett's are just two cases out of many. Other famous names connected with Chinese textile acquisitions are Gertrude Jekyll (1843–1932), the gifted plantswoman (V&A T.120-1916), and Bernard Leach (1887–1979), perhaps the most influential figure in the studio pottery movement of the twentieth century (V&A T.117 to T.122-

124 Album of embroidered Lohans
1850–1900
Page size 20 x 23 cm
V&A: T.74-1971

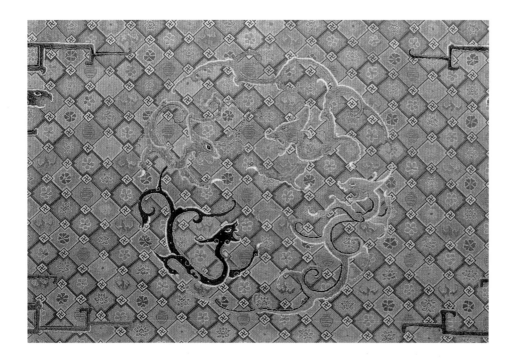

125 Embroidered silk table
frontal (detail of plate 41)
V&A: FE.37-1911

1958). In 1911 Roger Fry (1866–1934), one of the leading art critics of his day as well as
a philosopher and painter, sold the museum a beautifully executed piece of Chinese
embroidery, a table frontal with spotted, sinuous dragons superimposed over a ground of
counted thread stitches (plate 125). Of interest here is the lack of recorded information
within the museum concerning Fry's ownership of such a fine piece. The archive does tell
us, however, about the connections that were established following on the transaction.
Fry and the first Keeper of the V&A's Department of Textiles, Albert Frank Kendrick
(1872–1954), struck a gentlemanly deal of thirty pounds
for the frontal, and very soon after, Roger Fry was inviting
Kendrick to view the contemporary textiles being made at
his Omega Workshop in Fitzroy Square, London.[8]

126 Embroidered silk
wedding chair curtain
1910–20
45.5 x 65 cm
V&A: T.44-1952
Given by Sir Steven Runciman

The 1952 textile gifts of Sir Steven Runciman
(1903–2000), the great historian of the Crusades, are rather
special, regardless of the renown of the donor. A woman's
yellow court robe (V&A T.43-1956), unique within the
V&A and rare anywhere, plus an entire set of wedding
palanquin drapes and cushions, make up the donation. One
curtain from this almost pristine set is illustrated in plate
126. At a traditional Chinese wedding, the bride travels in
an enclosed chair or carriage and is completely hidden from
view. We presume that Runciman acquired these
embroideries in China. There is, however, no mention in
the museum records of his tour there in 1925 and certainly
no reference to his playing piano duets with the last

emperor, Puyi (1906–76, r.1908–12).[9] What the records do reveal, once again, is the camaraderie between upper class men of the British establishment.[10]

Several women donors are also very much part of our story. In 1974 Joan Evans (1893–1977), a major benefactor to the V&A, offered the museum twenty-one large-scale Chinese textiles (V&A FE.109 to FE.122-1974). The women's festival hanging on page 69 is one of them and the flower-filled embroidery from the twentieth century (plate 127) is another. Over the years, she gave the museum quantities of European medieval and Renaissance jewellery and metalwork, and it was in this area that she published. She is not primarily remembered for her interest in things Chinese. She does not seem to have visited China and we know she purchased all the textiles at Liberty's, the aesthete's favourite department store in London's Regent Street. Such shops were not an uncommon source for museum acquisitions, especially those relating to Asia.[11]

Two names that signal a change of emphasis regarding Chinese textile acquisitions by the V&A are Bernard Vuilleumier (1897–?1948) and W. Llewellyn Jones (d.1949). Both of them concentrated their collecting endeavours exclusively on the textile arts of China. The museum purchased eighty-three separate items from Vuilleumier's estate after his early death (V&A T.81 to T.253-1948). Presented here is a tapestry hanging with Daoist emblems (plate 128) from his collection. It is not known how Vuilleumier, a Swiss banker, built up his collection. He apparently never travelled to China, and because of his premature demise the museum correspondence was conducted with lawyers and bankers handling his will. Consequently, the Vuilleumier archival record is a business transaction and tells us little about the background to either the collector himself or his collection.[12]

While we may not know much about Vuilleumier's contacts and the sources for his purchases, we get a strong sense of the reason why he collected such material. He was passionate about unravelling the meanings that lay behind the textiles' decorative motifs. Although he was by no means the first person to view Chinese objects from this perspective, his lectures, exhibitions and publications on what he termed 'symbolism' caught the public imagination and nurtured its interest like no other, so that this theme remains, to this day, an abiding preoccupation for many visitors to the V&A (plate 129).

127 Embroidered silk hanging or cover
1900–1930
93 x 240 cm
V&A: FE.117-1974
Given by Joan Evans

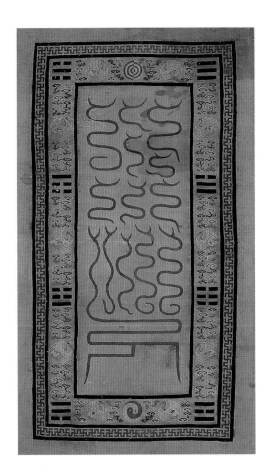

128 Picture of tapestry woven
silk, Daoist emblems
*c.*1750–1900
80 x 45 cm
V&A: T.164-1948
Vuilleumier Collection,
purchased with a grant from the
National Art Collections Fund

129 Bernard Vuilleumier
in London, 1939
The Swiss collector is pictured
at the opening of an exhibition
of his Chinese textiles and robes
held at the China Institute in
Gordon Square. The label for
the Daoist tapestry reads,
somewhat fancifully, 'Magic
Daoist Picture of Protection
for the Son of Heaven'.

The delicately embroidered picture in plate 130 is from the Llewellyn Jones bequest.
It depicts one of the manifestations of Liu Hai, the God of Wealth. Here he appears as a
child, beguiling in a feather cape and leaf skirt, punting along on a lotus boat which is
also being towed by a spotted, three-legged toad. Like several other pieces we have looked
at, this might be a mirror cover for a bridal chamber, both the boy immortal and the
lotuses being appropriate motifs for weddings.

Papers relating to the Llewellyn Jones bequest, some twenty items (V&A T.744 to
T.765-1950), among which is a rare yellow twelve-symbol court robe, give no indication
whatsoever of why this Guernsey resident became interested in Chinese textiles in
particular, nor very much information on how he acquired them. He was aware of
Bernard Vuilleumier's venture and purchased a few of the Swiss collector's pieces.

The museum archives do give us an insight into the complications that sizeable
collections of stuff can create for collectors and their heirs. The correspondence of 1945
comes from Cheshire, where Llewellyn Jones was preparing to return home to Guernsey
after the German occupation of the island and the requisitioning of his house during the
Second World War (1939–45). His collection, hidden away for the duration of the war,
survived intact. On his death in 1949 some of the pieces, chosen by the collector himself,
came to the museum. They were considerably delayed by the London dock strike of

130 Embroidered silk picture
with seed pearls
1840–1900
93 x 59 cm
V&A: T.762-1950
Llewellyn Jones Bequest

131 Pair of embroidered silk
cushion covers
1970–80
D. 50 cm
V&A: FE.124-1983
Addis Bequest

March 1949 although they were eventually entered in the museum's daybook in 1950. A detailed catalogue, mentioned by the donor's son as having been compiled by his father, was never forthcoming.[13]

A career in the diplomatic service gave many people the opportunity to study and collect artefacts of all kinds in the countries where they were posted. The previously discussed set of Buddhist tapestries (pages 47 and 48) was originally mounted in a specially made frame commissioned by the Belgian ambassador to China and his wife around 1915, and subsequently displayed in their various houses as interior decoration, as well as being loaned for exhibition.[14]

Museums have greatly benefited from diplomats' local knowledge as well as from generous donations and bequests of objects. Sir John Addis (1914–83) is not usually associated with textiles, although he is well known to specialists for his pre-eminent collections of Chinese porcelain and furniture, which he bequeathed to the British Museum and the V&A. This distinguished British diplomat and scholar also had a varied group of Chinese and other textiles stored in a handsome camphor wood chest, and this was transferred to the V&A from the family home in Kent, in south-east England, after his death. There are no surviving notes about the textiles from his hand; still less did he ever publish or publicly display them.

The Addis textile collection consists of both historic and contemporary items. The bright blue cushion covers (plate 131), hand embroidered with peonies and birds, have been given a date between 1970 and 1980. Furnishing accessories like these were produced in large quantities during this period and such pieces appear in Chinese overseas trade catalogues of the time. Sir John Addis may have been given them as a gift or he may have bought them at a trade fair or embroidery workshop. In many respects, the Addis textiles are a collection of souvenirs. They proved irresistible for a man who manifestly enjoyed the visual and who had the leisure and opportunity to shop for such pieces.[15]

Although it does not proclaim itself as such, the V&A is in part a repository for souvenirs and, like the Addis pieces, many of the textiles in the museum came from China as mementoes. By and large, small groups or single donations make up the bulk of the Chinese textile collection, and these were mostly given, and sometimes sold, to the V&A by descendants of people who had benefited from shopping opportunities either within Asia itself or in 'oriental bazaars' at home.

While it is true that during the foreigners' heyday for shopping in China, in the period spanning the end of the nineteenth century and the first three decades of the twentieth century, both dealer and customer often set great store by such markers as age and imperial connections, this should be tempered with the view of many that they were buying something to take home that was, above all, decorative and unmistakably Chinese. This view is borne out by descriptions of shops and markets of the time, and Juliet Bredon, a long-time resident of Beijing and one of the city's most diligent foreign recorders, speaks for all when she describes Beijing shopping as a never-failing source of interest and amusement.

Bredon, whose classic work on Beijing was first published in 1919 and reprinted and enlarged throughout the 1920s and 30s, conceded that by the 1930s the supply of fine throne covers, tapestry pictures, brocades, cut velvets and court gowns that were stolen or sold from imperial palaces, or left unredeemed in pawnshops by poor Manchus, was drying up, having been avidly purchased by 'world-girdlers', as she termed them. She also mentioned that reproductions of silk tapestry and throne cushions especially were sold as genuine antiques, a sentiment echoed by the Cook's *Guide to Peking*, which also reported the widespread practice of cutting, reshaping and gluing old garments into saleable tourist items.[16] There are many pieces of this type in the V&A.

For part of the period under discussion, when tourism was at one of its peaks in the first half of the twentieth century, Beijing was not the capital of China. The attitude of both its residents and its tourists was one of heightened nostalgia for its imperial past, and this sentiment manifested itself in a search for old artefacts connected with this fabled history and accounts for a lot of what is in the V&A's Chinese textile collection today.[17]

The V&A's collection was not on the whole enriched by Christian missionaries, a source of many so-called 'ethnographic' holdings.[18] There are, however, some items in the museum that might be categorized that way. The Hoklo banner (plate 132) came from Valery Garrett, whose collecting cut across several categories to embrace rural and urban Chinese textiles of the twentieth century.

By 1995, when the V&A was fortunate enough to secure a large section of Mrs Garrett's collection, curators were aware of the shifting nature of categorization and were well able to justify such an acquisition. Along with the other donors that have been mentioned – Bock, Forrer, Stein and Vuilleumier – Valery Garrett belongs to that group of collectors and dealers who wrote up their material before passing it on to the V&A, a pattern that runs through the entire museum collections and extends back to the nineteenth century.[19]

132 Celebratory banner
Cotton, sequins, braid, beads
Inscription: 'Safe and Prosperous'
1950–80
43 x 98 cm
V&A: FE.251-1995
Garrett Collection, purchased with a grant from the Friends of the V&A
This banner was used by the Hoklo people, a group originally from the southern coastal regions of China.

NOTES

CHAPTER 1
1 For a history of the V&A and its collections see Anthony Burton, *Vision and Accident: The Story of the Victoria and Albert Museum* (London: V&A Publications, 1999), especially chapters 5 and 10, figure 10.9; for a comparison with the V&A see Christa C. Mayer Thurman, 'Introduction' in 'Clothed to Rule the Universe: Ming and Qing Dynasty Textiles at The Art Institute of Chicago', *Museum Studies*, 26.2 (2000), 6–11.
2 James C.Y. Watt and Anne E. Wardwell, *When Silk Was Gold: Central Asian and Chinese Textiles*, exhibition catalogue (New York: The Metropolitan Museum of Art/The Cleveland Museum of Art, 1997).
3 Jonathan D. Spence, *The Search for Modern China* (London: Hutchinson, 1990), pp.170–84; Jonathan D. Spence, *God's Chinese Son: The Taiping Heavenly Kingdom of Hong Xiuquan* (New York: W.W. Norton, 1996).
4 Ian Heath and Michael Perry, *The Taiping Rebellion 1851–66*, Osprey Men-At-Arms Series, 275 (London: Osprey, 1994).
5 W*ith Gordon in China: Letters from Thomas Lyster*, edited by E.A. Lyster (London: Fisher Unwin, 1891), p.149; *Gordon's Campaign in China*, by Himself with an Introduction and Short Account of the Tai-Ping Rebellion by Colonel R.H. Vetch (London: Chapman Hall, 1900), pp.42–3, originally written by Gordon in *The Professional Papers of the Corps of Royal Engineers*, 19 (1871).
6 Austin Coats, *China Races* (Hong Kong: Oxford University Press, 1983), pp.22, 27–43, 258; Frances Wood, *No Dogs and Not Many Chinese: Treaty Port Life in China 1843–1943* (London: John Murray, 1998), pp.26, 225–6.
7 Anna Jackson, 'Art and Design: East Asia', in *The Victorian Vision: Inventing New Britain*, edited by John M. Mackenzie, exhibition catalogue (London: V&A Publications, 2001), pp. 297–313

(p.302 and plate 289).
8 *Chinese Export Art and Design*, edited by Craig Clunas (London: Victoria and Albert Museum, 1987); Richard Dunn and Anthony Burton, 'The Victoria and Albert Museum: An Illustrated Chronology', in *A Grand Design: The Art of the Victoria and Albert Museum*, edited by Malcolm Baker and Brenda Richardson, exhibition catalogue (London: V&A Publications, 1997), pp.48–77; Craig Clunas, 'The Imperial Collections: East Asian Art', in *A Grand Design*, pp.230–7, 260, plate 106.

CHAPTER 2
1 Dieter Kuhn, *Science and Civilisation in China*, edited by Joseph Needham, vol.5, Chemistry and Chemical Technology, part IX, *Textile Technology: Spinning and Reeling* (Cambridge: Cambridge University Press, 1988), pp.272–8.
2 Sergei I. Rudenko, *Frozen Tombs of Siberia: The Pazyryk Burials of Iron-Age Horsemen* (London: Dent, 1970), pp.304–6; M.P. Zavitukhina, *Frozen Tombs: The Culture and Art of the Ancient Tribes of Siberia*, exhibition catalogue (London: British Museum Press, 1978), p.51 and plate 39.
3 John Becker, *Pattern and Loom: A Practical Study of the Development of Weaving Techniques in China, Western Asia and Europe*, plus a supplement of enlarged weaving drafts (Copenhagen: Rhodos, 1987), pp.237–45; Feng Zhao, *Treasures In Silk* (Hong Kong: ISAT/Costume Squad Ltd, 1999), pp.333–5.
4 Verity Wilson, 'Early Textiles from Central Asia: Approaches to Study with Reference to the Stein Loan Collection in the Victoria and Albert Museum, London', *Textile History*, 26.1 (May 1995), 23–52; Sarah E. Fraser, *Performing the Visual: The Practice of Buddhist Wall Painting in China and Central Asia, 618–960* (Stanford: Stanford University Press, 2004), pp.131–58.
5 *The Travels of an Alchemist: The*

Journey of the Taoist Ch'ang-Ch'un from China to the Hindukush at the Summons of Chingiz Khan, translated with an Introduction by Arthur Waley (London: Routledge, 1931), p.124; James C.Y. Watt and Anne E. Wardwell, *When Silk Was Gold: Central Asian and Chinese Silk*, exhibition catalogue (New York: The Metropolitan Museum of Art/The Cleveland Museum of Art, 1997), pp.130–1.
6 Verity Wilson, 'An Enthusiastic Cleric and Five Silk Fragments from China', *Oriental Art* (Summer 1998), 62–5.
7 Esin Atıl, *Renaissance of Islam: Art of the Mamluks*, exhibition catalogue (Washington D.C: Smithsonian Institution Press, 1981), pp.223–5, and plates 114, 116, 121.
8 William S. Atwell, 'Time, Money and the Weather: Ming China and the "Great Depression" of the Mid-Fifteenth Century', *Journal of Asian Studies*, 61.1 (2002), 83–114.
9 Verity Wilson, 'Chinese Silk for Scotland: The Ivory Damask Bed Curtains for Melville House, c.1700', *Transactions of the Oriental Ceramic Society* 66 (2001–2) 111–12; *Design and the Decorative Arts: Britain 1500–1900*, edited by Michael Snodin and John Styles (London: V&A Publications, 2001), pp.90–1.
10 *Design and the Decorative Arts*, pp.114–15.
11 C.J.A. Jörg, *Porcelain and the Dutch China Trade* (The Hague: Martinus Nijhoff, 1982), pp.94–112; David Sanctuary Howard, *Chinese Armorial Porcelain* (London: Faber and Faber, 1974), pp.917–26; Verity Wilson, 'Silk', in *Chinese Export Art and Design*, edited by Craig Clunas (London: Victoria and Albert Museum, 1987), pp.22–33; Museum Catharijneconvent, Utrecht, *Borduurkunst Uit China: Voortborduren op Oude Tradities*, exhibition catalogue (Utrecht: Museum Catharijneconvent 1995), pp.19–21.
12 G.F. Wingfield Digby, 'Some

Silks Woven Under Portuguese Influence in the Far East', *Burlington Magazine*, 77 (1940), 52–63; Verity Wilson, 'Celebrating Twenty-Five Years in the Far Eastern Collection of the Victoria and Albert Museum', *Orientations* (November 1995), 52–63 (p.61).
13 Craig Clunas, *Pictures and Visuality in Early Modern China* (London: Reaktion, 1997), pp.172–83.
14 Verity Wilson, 'Studio and Soirée: Chinese Textiles in Europe and America, 1850 to the Present', in *Unpacking Culture: Art and Commodity in Colonial and Postcolonial Worlds*, edited by Ruth B. Phillips and Christopher B. Steiner (Berkeley: University of California Press, 1999), pp.229–42 (pp.239–42); Carolina Stone, *Sevilla y los Mantones de Manila*, Colección Giralda 3 (Sevilla: Área de Cultura Ayuntamiento de Sevilla, n.d.).
15 Verity Wilson, 'Chinese Painted Silks for Export in the Victoria and Albert Museum', *Orientations* (October 1987), 30–5; *Design and the Decorative Arts*, pp.270–2.
16 Susan Naquin, *Peking: Temples and City Life, 1400–1900* (Berkeley: University of California Press, 2000), pp.686–702.
17 Sarah Cheang, 'The Ownership and Collection of Chinese Material Culture by Women in Britain, c.1890–c.1935' (unpublished Ph.D. dissertation, University of Sussex, 2003).
18 Gloria Granz Gonick, 'Imported Textiles in *Matsuri*', in *Matsuri! Japanese Festival Arts*, edited by Gloria Granz Gonick, exhibition catalogue (Los Angeles: UCLA Fowler Museum of Cultural History, 2002), pp.183–209 (pp.192–9); *Catalogue of the Kurashiki Museum of Folk Craft*, 3 vols (Kurashiki: 1988), III, pp.11, 84–5.
19 S. Wells Williams, *The Chinese Commercial Guide* (Hong Kong: A. Shortrede & Co, 1863), p.113.
20 V&A Archives and Registry, Langewis nominal file.

CHAPTER 3

1 Zhang Hongxing, *The Qianlong Emperor: Treasures from the Forbidden City*, exhibition catalogue (Edinburgh: National Museums of Scotland, 2002), pp.151, 157.
2 Craig Clunas, *Chinese Furniture*, Victoria and Albert Museum Far Eastern Series (London: Bamboo Publishing, 1988), pp.15–17.
3 Craig Clunas, *Chinese Furniture*, pp.29–31; *Chinese Art and Design: The T.T. Tsui Gallery of Chinese Art*, edited by Rose Kerr (London: Victoria and Albert Museum, 1991), pp.116–17, 126–9.
4 Verity Wilson, 'A Diplomat's Collection: The Chinese Textiles of Sir John Addis', *Arts of Asia*, 33.2 (2003), 90–101.
5 'A Study of Women and Girls in Industries in Tientsin', *Chinese Economic Journal*, 2 (June 1928), 519–28; Chao Kang, *The Development of Cotton Textile Production in China* (Cambridge, Mass: Harvard University Press, 1977), pp.28–31; Richard Kraus, *Cotton and Cotton Goods in China 1918–1936* (New York: Garland, 1980); Emily Honig, S*isters and Strangers: Women in the Shanghai Cotton Mills, 1919–1949* (Stanford: Stanford University Press, 1986).
6 Chao Kang, *The Development of Cotton Textile Production in China*, pp.248–9; Verity Wilson, 'Dress and the Cultural Revolution', in *China Chic: East Meets West*, edited by Valerie Steele and John S. Major (New Haven and London: Yale University Press, 1999), pp.166–86 (pp.176–7).
7 Lois Fisher, *Go Gently Through Peking: A Westerner's Life in China* (London: Souvenir Press, 1979), p.247.
8 Chang Shangren and Wen Lianchang, *Ranzhi Tu'an Jichu* (Fundamentals of Textile Design) (Shanghai, 1979).
9 *Chinese Art and Design*, pp.118–23; Craig Clunas, *Chinese Furniture*, p.100.
10 V&A Archives and Registry, Logan nominal file.
11 Chün-fang Yü, '*Guanyin*: The Chinese Transformation of Avalokiteshvara', in *Latter Days of the Law: Images of Chinese Buddhism, 850–1850*, edited by Marsha Weidner, exhibition catalogue, Spencer Museum of Art, University of Kansas (Lawrence and Honolulu: Spencer Museum/University of Hawaii Press, 1994), pp.151–81 (pp.152–3).
12 Craig Clunas, *Chinese Furniture*, pp.96–7.
13 Claudia Brown, *Weaving China's Past: The Amy S. Clague Collection of Chinese Textiles*, exhibition catalogue (Phoenix: Phoenix Art Museum, 2000), pp.88–91.
14 *Masterpieces of Chinese Silk Tapestry and Embroidery in the National Palace Museum* (Taipei: National Palace Museum, 1971), plates 4, 36, 37.
15 Shelagh Vainker, *Chinese Silk: A Cultural History* (London: British Museum Press, 2004), pp.131–7.
16 See illustrations from *Tuhua Ribao* and *Shenjiang shengjing tushuo* in Catherine Vance Yeh, 'Reinventing Ritual: Late Qing Handbooks for Proper Customer Behavior in Shanghai Courtesan Houses', *Late Imperial China* (December 1998), 1–63.
17 Lothar Ledderose, *Ten Thousand Things: Module and Mass Production in Chinese Art*, The A.W. Mellon Lectures in the Fine Arts, 1998, The National Gallery of Art, Washington, D.C., Bollingen Series XXXV: 45 (Princeton: Princeton University Press, 2000), pp.6–7.
18 Stephen W. Bushell, *Chinese Art*, 2 vols (London: HMSO, 1924), II, p.101 and figure 121.
19 Chen Juanjuan, 'Shen Shou jiqi cixiu "Liu yan tu"' (Shen Shou and Her Embroidery 'Willows and Swallows'), *Gugong Bowuyuan Yuankan* (April, 1983), 45–6; *Threads of Light: Chinese Embroidery from Suzhou and the Photography of Robert Glenn Ketchum*, edited by Patrick Dowdy, exhibition catalogue (Los Angeles: Fowler Museum of Cultural History, 1999), pp.41–6; Grace S. Fong, 'Female Hands: Embroidery as a Knowledge Field in Women's Everyday Life in Late Imperial and Early Republican China', *Late Imperial China* (June 2004), 1–58.

20 *Nichols Super Yarn and Carpets: The Story of Nichols Chinese Rugs* (n.d.); Alix H. Perrachon, 'The Vogue of the Chinese Carpet: The Peking and Tientsin Era', *Hali*, 5.2 (1982), 149–55; Margaret Setton, 'Chinese Rugs: The Fetti-Li Company', *Oriental Rug Review*, 4.8 (1984), 13–22.
21 Julia F. Andrews, 'Commercial Art and China's Modernisation', in *A Century in Crisis, Modernity and Tradition in the Art of Twentieth-Century China*, edited by Julia F. Andrews and Kuiyi Shen, exhibition catalogue (New York: Guggenheim Museum, 1998), pp.181–97 (pp.185–6).
22 Michael Franses and Robert Pinner, 'Chinese Carpets in the Victoria and Albert Museum', *Hali*, 5.2 (1982), 141–8.
23 Charles I. Rostov and Jia Guanyin with Li Linpan and Zhang H.Z., *Chinese Carpets* (New York: Harry N. Abrahams Inc, 1983), pp.72–81.
24 Brian Spooner, 'Weavers and Dealers: The Authenticity of an Oriental Carpet', in *The Social Life of Things: Commodities in Cultural Perspectives*, edited by Arjun Appadurai (Cambridge: Cambridge University Press, 1986), pp.195–235.
25 R.H. van Gulik, *Chinese Pictorial Art as Viewed by the Connoisseur*, Serie Orientale Roma, 19 (Rome: Istituto Italiano Per Il Medio Estremo Oriente, 1958); Zhang Hongxing, *The Qianlong Emperor*, pp.34–5, 55, 61, 86; Shelagh Vainker, *Chinese Silk*, pp.146–8.

CHAPTER 4

1 Jane Schneider, 'The Anthropology of Cloth', *Annual Review of Anthropology* (1987), 409–48.
2 For early grave silks found at Mashan and Mawangdui see Shelagh Vainker, *Chinese Silk: A Cultural History* (London: British Museum Press, 2004), pp.37–40, 48–53; for SunYat-sen's 1929 coffin drape see Li Xiangshu, *Xiang xiu shihua* (The History of Xiang Embroidery) (Beijing: Qing gongye chubanshe, 1988), pp.82–6.
3 Jerome Silbergeld, 'Chinese Concepts of Old Age and Their Role in Chinese Painting, Painting Theory, and Criticism', *Art Journal* (Summer 1987), 103–14 (pp.107–8).
4 *Chinese Art and Design: The T.T. Tsui Gallery of Chinese Art*, edited by Rose Kerr (London: Victoria and Albert Museum, 1991), pp.214–15.
5 S.I. Hsiung, *Lady Precious Stream: An Old Chinese Play Done into English According to its Traditional Style* (London: Methuen, 1934); Mei Lanfang, *Wutai shenghuo sishi nian* (Forty Years on the Stage), 3 vols (Shanghai: Pingming chubanshe, 1953–1954); Graham Russell Gao Hodges, *Anna May Wong: From Laundryman's Daughter to Hollywood Legend* (New York: Palgrave Macmillan, 2004); James Laver, *Museum Piece or the Education of an Iconographer* (London: André Deutsch, 1963), p.120.
6 V&A Archives and Registry, Stewart Lockhart nominal file; Susan Leiper, *Precious Cargo: Scots and the China Trade*, exhibition catalogue (Edinburgh: National Museums of Scotland, 1997), pp.79–80.
7 Wang Yan, *Wanli dihou de yichu: Ming Dingling sizhi jijin* (The Wanli Emperor's Wardrobe: The Textiles of the Dingling Tomb) (Taibei: Dongdu tushu gongsi, 1995), pp. 83–107, 220–31.
8 Terese Tse Bartholomew, 'One Hundred Children: From Boys at Play to Icons of Good Fortune', in *Children in Chinese Art*, edited by Ann Barrott Wicks (Honolulu: University of Hawai'i Press, 2002), pp.57–83; for an early depiction of boys see Wu Hung, 'Private Love and Public Duty: Images of Children in Early Chinese Art', in *Chinese Views of Childhood*, edited by Anne Behnke Kinney (Honolulu: University of Hawai'i Press, 1995), pp.79–110; for a twentieth-century view see Stephanie Donald, 'Children as Political Messengers: Art, Childhood, Continuity', in *Picturing Power in the People's Republic of China: Posters of the Cultural Revolution*, edited by Harriet Evans and

Stephanie Donald (Lanham, Maryland: Rowman and Littlefield, 1999), pp.79–100.

9 Susan Mann, 'The Male Bond in Chinese History and Culture', *American Historical Review,* AHR Forum, 'Gender and Manhood in Chinese History' (December 2000), 1599–1614.

10 Terese Tse Bartholomew, *The Hundred Flowers: Botanical Motifs in Chinese Art* (San Francisco: Asian Art Museum, 1985), plate 45; Terese Tse Bartholomew, *Myths and Rebuses in Chinese Art* (San Francisco: Asian Art Museum, 1988), unpaginated, pp.8–11.

11 G. William Skinner, 'Creolized Chinese Societies in Southeast Asia', in *Sojourners and Settlers: Histories of Southeast Asia and the Chinese,* edited by Anthony Read (Honolulu: University of Hawai'i Press, 2001, first published 1996), pp.51–93; Khoo Joo Ee, *The Straits Chinese: A Cultural History* (Amsterdam and Kuala Lumpur: Pepin Press, 1996).

12 Ho Wing Meng, *Straits Chinese Beadwork and Embroidery: A Collector's Guide* (Singapore: Times Books International, 1987); Eng-Lee Seok Chee, *Festive Expressions: Nonya Beadwork and Embroidery* (Singapore: National Museum of Singapore, 1989).

13 Carl Schuster, 'An Archaic Form of Chess Game in Chinese Peasant Embroidery', *Man* (September 1936), 148–51; Andrew Lo, 'Dice, Dominoes and Card Games in Chinese Literature: A Preliminary Survey' in *Chinese Studies,* edited by Frances Wood, British Library Occasional Papers 10 (London: British Library, 1988), 127–35 and personal communication with Andrew Lo, School of Oriental and African Studies, University of London.

14 Catherine Pagani, 'From Woodblock to Textile: Imagery of Elite Culture in the Blue-and-White Embroideries of Sichuan', *Revue d'art canadienne/Canadian Art Review* 24.1 (1997), 28–41; Iris Wachs, *Magical Shapes: Twentieth Century Chinese Papercuts,* exhibition catalogue, in English and Hebrew (Tel Aviv: Eretz Israel

Museum, 2004), pp.15–17, 54–5, plate 22, 119, plates 89 and 90.

15 Tanya Harrod, ' "For Love and Not For Money": Reviving "Peasant Art" in Britain 1880–1930', in *The Lost Arts of Europe: The Haslemere Collection of European Peasant Art,* edited by David Crowley and Lou Taylor, exhibition catalogue (Haslemere, Surrey: Haslemere Educational Museum, 2000), pp.13–24.

16 Carl Schuster, 'A Bird Motif in Chinese Peasant Embroidery' (Peking, 1936) n.p., translated from Josef Strzygowski, *Spuren Indogermanischen Glaubens in der bildenden Kunst* (Heidelberg, 1936), pp.326–44; Carl Schuster and Edmund Carpenter, *Patterns That Connect: Social Symbolism in Ancient and Tribal Art* (New York: Harry N. Abrams, 1996).

17 Ann Waltner, 'Recent Scholarship on Chinese Women', *Signs* (Winter 1996), 410–28; Susan Mann, 'The History of Chinese Women Before the Age of Orientalism', *Journal of Women's History* (Winter 1997), 163–76; Grace S. Fong, 'Female Hands: Embroidery as a Knowledge Field in Women's Everyday Life in Late Imperial and Early Republican China', *Late Imperial China* (June 2004), 1–58.

18 *Chinese Art and Design,* pp.70–111; Verity Wilson, 'Cosmic Raiment: Daoist Traditions of Liturgical Clothing', *Orientations* (May 1995), 42–9.

19 T. Griffith Foulk, 'Religious Functions of Buddhist Art in China', in *Cultural Intersections in Later Chinese Buddhism,* edited by Marsha Weidner (Honolulu: University of Hawai'i Press, 2001), pp.13–29.

20 Terese Tse Bartholomew, '*Thangkas* for the Qianlong Emperor's Seventieth Birthday', in *Cultural Intersections,* pp.170–88; *Latter Days of the Law: Images of Chinese Buddhism 850–1850,* edited by Marsha Weidner, exhibition catalogue (Honolulu: University of Hawaii Press, 1994); Patricia Berger, *Empire of Emptiness: Buddhist Art and Political Authority in Qing China* (Honolulu: University of Hawai'i Press, 2003).

21 For the Great Leap Forward see Jonathan D. Spence, *The Search for Modern China* (London: Hutchinson, 1990), pp.574–83; for Picasso's peace dove see Li Xiangshu, *Xiang xiu shihua,* p.107 and David Caute, *The Dancer Defects: The Struggle for Cultural Supremacy During the Cold War* (Oxford: Oxford University Press, 2003), pp.580, 721 n.45; for the accordion see http://www.accordions.com/index/his/his_cn.shtml.

22 Lois Fisher, *Go Gently Through Peking: A Westerner's Life in China* (London: Souvenir Press, 1979), pp.170–1.

CHAPTER 5

1 Sophie Desrosiers, 'Une culture textile raffinée' and 'Une culture du textile', in *Keriya, mémoires d'un fleuve: Archéologie et Civilisation des Oasis de Taklamakan,* edited by Corinne Debaine-Francfort and Abduressul Idriss, Mission archéologique franco-chinoise au Xinjiang (Suilly-la-Tour and Paris: Editions Findakly/Foundation EDF, 2001), pp.144–55 (pp.145–6), pp.177–213 (pp.190–7).

2 Craig Clunas, *Superfluous Things: Material Culture and Social Status in Early Modern China* (Cambridge: Polity Press, 1991), pp.46–9.

3 Verity Wilson, *Chinese Dress,* Victoria and Albert Museum Far Eastern Series (London: Victoria and Albert Museum, 1986), pp.12–29; Verity Wilson, 'Studio and Soirée: Chinese Textiles in Europe and America, 1850 to the Present', in *Unpacking Culture: Art and Commodity in Colonial and Postcolonial Worlds,* edited by Ruth B. Phillips and Christopher B. Steiner (Berkeley: University of California Press, 1999), pp.229–42.

4 *Chinese Art: Autumn Exhibition, 1913,* exhibition catalogue (London: Whitechapel Art Gallery, 1913).

5 Verity Wilson, 'A Diplomat's Collection: The Chinese Textiles of Sir John Addis', *Arts of Asia,* 33.2 (2003), 90–101.

6 Verity Wilson, *Chinese Dress,* pp.100–1; Verity Wilson, 'A

Diplomat's Collection' (p.93).

7 Richard Kraus, *Cotton and Cotton Goods in China 1918–1936* (New York: Garland, 1980), p.123; Henrietta Harrison, *The Making of the Republican Citizen: Political Ceremonies and Symbols in China, 1911–1929* (Oxford: Oxford University Press, 2000), pp.49–83; Karl Gerth, *China Made: Consumer Culture and the Creation of the Nation* (Cambridge, Mass: Harvard University Press, 2003), pp.68–121.

8 Antonia Finnane, 'What Should Chinese Women Wear? A National Problem', *Modern China* 22.2 (1996), 99–131; Ellen Johnston Laing, 'Visual Evidence for the Evolution of "Politically Correct" Dress for Women in Early Twentieth Century Shanghai', *Nan Nü* 5.1 (2003), 69–114.

9 Ellen Johnston Laing, 'Visual Evidence' (pp.104–5).

10 Naomi Yin-yin Szeto, *Of Hearts and Hands: Hong Kong's Traditional Trades and Crafts,* Hong Kong Museum of History (Hong Kong: Urban Council of Hong Kong, 1996), pp.66–7; Ellen Johnston Laing, 'Visual Evidence' (pp.91–101).

11 Francesca Dal Lago, 'Crossed Legs in 1930s Shanghai: How "Modern" the Modern Woman', *East Asian History* (June 2000), 103–44; Ellen Johnston Laing, 'Visual Evidence' (pp.105–6).

12 Naomi Yin-yin Szeto, *Of Hearts and Hands,* pp.68–9.

13 Verity Wilson, 'Dressing for Leadership in China: Wives and Husbands in an Age of Revolutions (1911–1976)', *Gender and History* (November 2002), 608–28; Ellen Johnston Laing, 'Visual Evidence' (pp.99–101).

14 Geremie R. Barmé, *Shades of Mao: The Posthumous Cult of the Great Leader* (Armonk, NY: M.E. Sharpe, 1996), pp.46,102–3; *China Chic: East Meets West* edited by Valerie Steele and John S. Major (New Haven and London: Yale University Press, 1999), plate 1, pp.89–91; Vivienne Tam with Martha Huang, *China Chic* (New York: Regan Books, 2000), pp.81–94.

15 Dieter Kuhn, *Science and Civilisation in China*, edited by Joseph Needham, vol.5, Chemistry and Chemical Technology, part IX, *Textile Technology: Spinning and Reeling* (Cambridge: Cambridge University Press, 1988), pp.15–30; Naomi Yin-yin Szeto, *Of Hearts and Hands*, pp.96–7; Gina Corrigan, *Miao Textiles from China* (London: British Museum Press, 2001), p.12 & bibliography.

16 C.W. Howard and K.P. Buswell, *A Survey of the Silk Industry of South China*, Agricultural Bulletin Number 12, Ling Nan Agricultural College, Department of Sericulture (Hong Kong: Commercial Press, 1925), p.156; Valery M. Garrett, *Traditional Chinese Clothing in Hong Kong and South China, 1840–1980*, Images of Asia Series (Hong Kong: Oxford University Press, 1987), pp.72–3.

17 Rudolph P. Hommel, *China At Work: An Illustrated Record of the Primitive Industries of China's Masses Whose Life is Toil, and thus an Account of Chinese Civilization* (New York: John Day, 1937, reprinted Cambridge, Mass: M.I.T. Press, 1969), p.191, figure 278; Valery M. Garrett, *Traditional Chinese Clothing*, p.75 after E.Watson, *The Principal Articles of Chinese Commerce* (Shanghai, 1930)); Valery M. Garrett, *Chinese Clothing: An Illustrated Guide* (Hong Kong: Oxford University Press, 1994), pp.108–9; Jenny Balfour-Paul, *Indigo* (London: British Museum Press, 1998), pp.134–9; Gina Corrigan, *Miao Textiles*, pp.14–15.

18 Valery M. Garrett, *Traditional Chinese Clothing*, pp.1–8.

19 Jenny Balfour-Paul, *Indigo*, pp.84, 94, 97, 108–9, 177, 197.

20 Verity Wilson, 'A Diplomat's Collection' (pp.96–7).

CHAPTER 6

1 For stitches and their various names in English and Chinese see Verity Wilson, *Chinese Dress*, Victoria and Albert Museum Far Eastern Series (London: Victoria and Albert Museum, 1986), pp.101–14; Wang Yarong, *Chinese Embroidery: A World of Fable and Colour* (Tokyo and New York: Kodansha, 1987), pp.129–5; Feng Zhao, *Treasures in Silk* (Hong Kong: ISAT/The Costume Squad, 1999), pp.343–7; *Threads of Light: Chinese Embroidery from Suzhou and the Photography of Robert Glenn Ketchum*, edited by Patrick Dowdy, exhibition catalogue (Los Angeles: Fowler Museum of Cultural History, 1999), pp.101–4; Feng Zhao, 'The Chronological Development of Needlelooping Embroidery', *Orientations* (February 2000), 44–53; Jocelyn Chatterton, *Chinese Silks and Sewing Tools* (London: Jocelyn Chatterton, 2002), pp.44–7, 74–81; Josiane Bertin-Guest, *Chinese Embroidery: Traditional Techniques* (Iola, WI: Krause, 2003), pp.43–19); Young Yang Chung, *Silken Threads: A History of Embroidery in China, Korea, Japan and Vietnam* (New York: Abrams, 2005).

2 *Chinese Art and Design: The T.T. Tsui Gallery of Chinese Art*, edited by Rose Kerr (London: Victoria and Albert Museum, 1991), pp.114–16.

3 'Soochow Embroidery', *Chinese Economic Journal* (February 1928), 163–5; 'The Embroidery Industry in Shanghai', *The China Journal* (May 1939), 267–8; H.C. Faulder, 'Embroidery in China', *China Exporter* (October 1939), 15; Li Xiangshu, *Xiang xiu shihua* (The History of Xiang Embroidery) (Beijing: Qing gongye chubanshe, 1988).

4 Craig Clunas, *Art in China*, Oxford History of Art (Oxford: Oxford University Press, 1997), pp.185–6.

5 'The Embroidery Industry in Shanghai'; Harriet Rietveld, 'Women and Children in Industry in Chefoo', *Chinese Economic Monthly* (December 1926), 559–62; Verity Wilson, *Chinese Dress*, pp.61–2, 105–6; Francesca Bray, *Technology and Gender: Fabrics of Power in Late Imperial China* (Berkeley: University of California Press, 1997), pp.206–69; Susan Mann, *Precious Records: Women in China's Long Eighteenth Century* (Stanford: Stanford University Press, 1997), pp.143–77; Noël Golvers, *François de Rougemont, S.J., Missionary in Ch'ang-shu (Chiang-nan): A Study of the Account Book (1674–1676), and the Elogium*, Louvain Chinese Studies VII (Louvain: Catholic University of Louvain, 1999), pp.541–2.

6 Herbert A. Carter, *Ramie (rhea) China Grass: The New Textile Fibre, All About It: A Book for Planters, Manufacturers, and Merchants* (London: Technical Publishing, 1910); 'Note on ramie weaving centres in Kiangsi', *Chinese Economic Bulletin* (March 1926), 144; 'Ramie and grasscloth of Kiangsi, *Chinese Economic Journal and Bulletin* (December 1936), 646–54.

7 United States Department of Commerce and Labor, 'Note on Swatow Drawn-work', by Consul A.W. Gilbert, Chefoo, *Monthly Consular and Trade Reports*, 349 (October 1909), 154; United States Department of Commerce, 'Drawn-work, Embroidery, and Lace Industries in Swatow District', *Commerce Reports*, 20 (25 January 1921), 478–80.

8 Naomi Yin-yin Szeto, *Of Hearts and Hands: Hong Kong's Traditional Trades and Crafts*, Hong Kong Museum of History (Hong Kong: Urban Council of Hong Kong, 1996), pp.64–5.

9 Lothar Ledderose, *Ten Thousand Things: Module and Mass Production in Chinese Art*, The A.W. Mellon Lectures in the Fine Arts, 1998, The National Gallery of Art, Washington, D.C., Bollingen Series XXXV: 45 (Princeton: Princeton University Press, 2000), pp.75–101; Henry Glassie, *The Potter's Art* (Bloomington: Indiana University Press, 1999), pp.96–8.

10 Leanna Lee-Whitman and Maruta Skelton, 'Where Did All the Silver Go? Identifying Chinese Painted and Printed Silks', *Textile Museum Journal*, 22 (1983), 33–52; Verity Wilson, 'Chinese Painted Silks for Export in the Victoria and Albert Museum', *Orientations* (October 1987), 30–5.

11 The periodical, *Folklore Studies*, published by the Museum of Oriental Ethnology, the Catholic University of Beijing, from the 1930s to the early 1950s, had contributions from both Chinese and European scholars; Ai Qing, *Minjian yishu he yiren* (Folk Art and Artists) (Beijing: Xinhua shudian, 1946); Shen Congwen, *Landi baibu de lishi fa zhan* (The History of the Development of Blue and White Cotton Textiles), *Wenwu cankao ziliao* (Cultural Relics Reference Material) (September 1958), 15–18; Laurence Schneider, *Ku Chieh-kang and China's New History: Nationalism and the Quest for Alternative Tradition* (Berkeley: University of California Press, 1971).

12 Rudolph P. Hommel, *China At Work: An Illustrated Record of the Primitive Industries of China's Masses Whose Life is Toil, and thus an Account of Chinese Civilization* (New York: John Day, 1937, reprinted Cambridge, Mass: M.I.T. Press, 1969), p.191, figure 278; Lin Hanjie, *Minjian lan yin huabu tuan* (Folk Blue Cloth Pictures) (Beijing: Renmin meishu chubanshe, 1953); Tseng Yu-ho Ecke, *Chinese Folk Art in American Collections: early 15th through early 20th centuries*, exhibition catalogue, China House Gallery (New York: China Institute in America, 1976), pp.34–41; Nancy Zeng Berliner, *Chinese Folk Art: The Small Skills of Carving Insects* (Boston: Little, Brown and Company, 1986), pp.180–95.

13 Carl Schuster, 'Stitch-Resist Dyed Fabrics of Western China', *Bulletin of the Needle and Bobbin Club*, 32 (1948), 10–29; Tseng Yu-ho Ecke, *Chinese Folk Art*, p.43; Gina Corrigan, *Miao Textiles from China* (London: British Museum Press, 2001), pp.16–17, 32–3, 39, 72–3; Feng Zhao, *Treasures in Silk*, p.348–9.

14 David M. Swann, 'British Cotton Mills in Pre-Second World War China', *Textile History*, 32.2 (2001), 195–200.

15 S. Sugiyama, 'Textile Marketing in East Asia, 1860–1914', in *The Textile Industries*, edited by S.D. Chapman, 2 vols (London: Tauris, 1997), II, Cotton: Linen: Wool and Worsted, pp.311–32.

16 James C.Y. Watt and Anne E. Wardwell, *When Silk Was Gold: Central Asian and Chinese Silk*, exhibition catalogue (New York: The Metropolitan Museum of Art/The Cleveland Museum of Art, 1997), pp.53–63.
17 Francesca Bray, *Technology and Gender*, p.191, n.23.
18 Irene Emery, *The Primary Structures of Fabrics: An Illustrated Classification* (Washington D.C: The Textile Museum, 1980); Dorothy K. Burnham, *Warp and Weft: A Textile Terminology* (Toronto: Royal Ontario Museum, 1980); Feng Zhao *Treasures in Silk*, pp.330–41.
19 Consul Bourne, *Trade of Central and Southern China* (Shanghai: Kelly and Walsh, 1898), p.28; Francesca Bray, *Technology and Gender*, p.209.
20 Sophie Desrosiers, 'La soierie méditerranéenne', *La Revue du Musée des Arts et Métiers*, 7 (1994), 51–8.
21 Francesca Bray, *Technology and Gender*, p.192, n.24.
22 C.W. Howard and K.P. Buswell, *A Survey of the Silk Industry of South China*, Agricultural Bulletin Number 12, Ling Nan Agricultural College, Department of Sericulture (Hong Kong: Commercial Press, 1925), pp.155–9; D.K. Lieu, *The Silk Industry of China* (Shanghai: Kelly and Walsh, 1941), pp.162–4; Lillian M. Li, *China's Silk Trade: Traditional Industry in the Modern World, 1842–1937* (Cambridge: Harvard University Press, 1981), pp.27, 29–30, 123, 163–8, 171.
23 Fang Ying-yang, 'Developing Dyestuffs', *China Reconstructs* (July 1957), 21–4 (p.21).
24 C.C. Chu and Thos. C. Blaisdell, Jr., *Peking Rugs and Peking Boys: A Study of the Rug Industry in Peking* (Peking: Chinese Social and Political Science Association, 1924), pp.8–9; Charles I. Rostov and Jia Guanyin with Li Linpan and Zhang H.Z., *Chinese Carpets* (New York: Harry N. Abrams Inc, 1983), pp.145, 207–8; Jon S. Ansari, 'Chinese Carpets: The Modernization of an Ancient Craft', *Hali*, 5.2 (1982), 156–8.
25 Alix H. Perrachon, 'The Vogue of the Chinese Carpet: The Peking and Tientsin Era', *Hali*, 5.2 (1982), 149–55 (p.151); Charles I. Rostov, *Chinese Carpets*, pp.206–7.
26 Charles I. Rostov, *Chinese Carpets*, pp.151–9; Marla Mallett, *Woven Structures: A Guide to Oriental Rug and Textile Analysis* (Atlanta: Christopher Publications and Marla Mallett Textiles, 1998); www.marlamallett.com; Jennifer Wearden, *Oriental Carpets and their Structure: Highlights from the V&A Collection* (London: V&A Publications, 2003), pp.7–23.
27 Chinese Carpets and Rugs Factory, *High-Grade Carpets & Rugs* (Shanghai: July 1921).
28 C.C. Chu and Thos. C. Blaisdell, Jr., *Peking Rugs and Peking Boys*; Margaret Setton, 'Chinese Rugs: The Fette-Li Company', *Oriental Rug Review* (November 1984), 13–22.

CHAPTER 7

1 For Great Exhibition acquisitions see Peter Trippi, 'Industrial Arts and the Exhibition Ideal', in *A Grand Design: The Art of the Victoria and Albert Museum*, edited by Malcolm Baker and Brenda Richardson (London: V&A Publications, 1997), pp.78–88; Anthony Burton, *Vision and Accident: The Story of the Victoria and Albert Museum* (London: V&A Publications, 1999), pp.31–2, 41–2, 44–5; for acquisitions from other exhibitions see Stephen W. Bushell, *Chinese Art*, 2 vols (London: HMSO, 1924), II, p.103 and figure 123; Anna Jackson, 'Art and Design: East Asia', in *The Victorian Vision: Inventing New Britain*, edited by John M. Mackenzie, exhibition catalogue (London: V&A Publications, 2001), pp.297–313 (pp.305–6 and plate 292).
2 V&A T.32 to T.34-1963 were purchased from Mr Wu Ying, the first Chinese name to appear in the archives; for a different view of Chinese textile collecting at the Art Institute of Chicago see Christa C. Mayer Thurman, 'Introduction' in 'Clothed to Rule the Universe: Ming and Qing Dynasty Textiles at The Art Institute of Chicago', *Museum Studies*, 26.2 (2000), pp.6–11 and Elinor Pearlstein, 'Color, Life and Moment: Early Chicago Collectors of Chinese Textiles' in the same volume, pp.80–93.
3 Verity Wilson, 'An Enthusiastic Cleric and Five Silk Fragments from China', *Oriental Art* (Summer 1998), 62–5.
4 Verity Wilson, 'Early Textiles from Central Asia: Approaches to Study with Reference to the Stein Loan Collection in the Victoria and Albert Museum, London', *Textile History*, 26.1 (May 1995), 23–52.
5 Judith Green, 'Britain's Chinese Collections: Private Collecting and the Invention of Chinese Art, 1842–1943' (unpublished Ph.D. dissertation, University of Sussex, 2003).
6 V&A Archives and Registry, Bluett nominal file; Stacey Pierson, 'Private Collecting, Teaching and Institutionalisation: the Percival David Foundation and the Field of Chinese Art in Britain, 1920–1964 (unpublished Ph.D. dissertation, University of Sussex, 2003).
7 http://www.fiveleaves.co.uk/ radical_bookselling.html compiled by Dave Cope and Ross Bradshaw; V&A Archives and Registry, Collet's nominal file; Christopher Wilk, 'Collecting the Twentieth Century', in *A Grand Design*, pp.345–53 (pp.349–50).
8 V&A Archives and Registry, Fry nominal file; *Art Made Modern: Roger Fry's Vision of Art*, edited by Christopher Green, exhibition catalogue (London: Courtauld Institute of Art /Merrell Holberton, 1999), pp.150–1; Judith Collins, 'Roger Fry's Social Vision of Art', in *Art Made Modern*, pp.73–84; Patricia Laurence, *Lily Briscoe's Chinese Eyes: Bloomsbury, Modernism, and China* (Columbia, South Carolina: University of South Carolina Press, 2003).
9 Steven Runciman, *A Traveller's Alphabet: Partial Memoirs* (New York: Thames and Hudson, 1991).
10 V&A Archives and Registry, Runciman nominal file.
11 Textiles belonging to Joan Evans appear in *International Exhibition of Chinese Art*, exhibition catalogue, Royal Academy of Arts (London: Royal Academy, third edition 1935–1936), pp.228, 230, 242, 247; Joan Evans, *Prelude and Fugue: An Autobiography* (London: Museum Press, 1964); for similar department store acquisitions in Chicago, USA see Christa C. Mayer Thurman, 'Clothed to Rule the Universe' (pp.9–11).
12 V&A Archives and Registry, Vuilleumier nominal file.
13 V&A Archives and Registry, Llewellyn Jones nominal file.
14 Personal meeting with Lady Logan, daughter of M. Robert-Gerard Everts.
15 Verity Wilson, 'A Diplomat's Collection: The Chinese Textiles of Sir John Addis', *Arts of Asia*, 33.2 (2003), 90–101.
16 *Peking and the Overland Route* (Shanghai: Thos. Cook & Son, 1917), p.23; Juliet Bredon, *Peking: A History and Intimate Description of Its Chief Places of Interest* (Shanghai: Kelly and Walsh, 1931), pp.443, 464–5.
17 Susan Naquin, *Peking: Temples and City Life, 1400–1900* (Berkeley: University of California Press, 2000), pp.679–708.
18 Judith Green, ' "Curiosity", "Art" and "Ethnography" in the Chinese Collections of John Henry Gray', in *Collectors: Individuals and Institutions*, edited by Anthony Shelton (London and Coimbra: Horniman Museum/Museu Antropológico da Universidade de Coimbra, 2001), pp.111–28; Nicky Levell, 'The Translation of Objects: R. and M. Davidson and the Friends' Foreign Mission Association, China, 1890–1894', in *Collectors: Individuals and Institutions*, pp.129–62.
19 Valery M. Garrett, *Traditional Chinese Clothing in Hong Kong and South China, 1840–1980*, Images of Asia Series (Hong Kong: Oxford University Press, 1987); Valery M. Garrett, *Chinese Clothing: An Illustrated Guide* (Hong Kong: Oxford University Press, 1994).

FURTHER READING

The Art Institute of Chicago, 'Clothed to Rule the Universe: Ming and Qing Dynasty Textiles at The Art Institute of Chicago', edited by Christa C. Mayer Thurman, *Museum Studies*, 26.2 (2000)

Muriel Baker and Margaret Lunt, *Blue and White: The Cotton Embroideries of Rural China* (London: Sidgwick and Jackson, 1978)

Josiane Bertin-Guest, *Chinese Embroidery: Traditional Techniques* (Iola, WI: Krause, 2003)

Fang Jing Pei, *Symbols and Rebuses in Chinese Art* (Berkeley and Toronto: Ten Speed Press, 2004)

Francesca Bray, *Technology and Gender: Fabrics of Power in Late Imperial China* (Berkeley: University of California Press, 1997)

Claudia Brown, *Weaving China's Past: The Amy S. Clague Collection of Chinese Textiles*, exhibition catalogue (Phoenix: Phoenix Art Museum, 2000)

Chinese Art and Design: The T.T. Tsui Gallery of Chinese Art, edited by Rose Kerr (London: Victoria and Albert Museum, 1991)

Chinese Export Art and Design, edited by Craig Clunas (London: Victoria and Albert Museum, 1987)

Young Yang Chung, *Silken Threads: A History of Embroidery in China, Korea, Japan and Vietnam* (New York: Abrams, 2005)

Fowler Museum of Cultural History, *Threads of Light: Chinese Embroidery from Suzhou and the Photography of Robert Glenn Ketchum*, edited by Patrick Dowdy, exhibition catalogue (Los Angeles: Fowler Museum of Cultural History, 1999)

Valery M. Garrett, *Traditional Chinese Clothing in Hong Kong and South China, 1840–1980*, Images of Asia Series (Hong Kong: Oxford University Press, 1987)

Valery M. Garrett, *A Collector's Guide to Chinese Dress Accessories* (Singapore: Times Editions, 1997)

Hong Kong Museum of Art, *Heaven's Embroidered Cloths: One Thousand Years of Chinese Textiles*, exhibition catalogue (Hong Kong: Urban Council of Hong Kong, 1995)

Robert D. Jacobsen, *Imperial Silks: Ch'ing Dynasty Textiles in the Minneapolis Institute of Arts*, 2 vols (Minneapolis: Minneapolis Institute of Arts, 2000)

Dorothy Ko, *Every Step A Lotus: Shoes For Bound Feet* (Berkeley: University of California Press/The Bata Shoe Museum Foundation, Toronto, 2001)

Dieter Kuhn, *Science and Civilisation in China*, edited by Joseph Needham, vol.5, Chemistry and Chemical Technology, part IX, *Textile Technology: Spinning and Reeling* (Cambridge: Cambridge University Press, 1988)

Charles I. Rostov and Jia Guanyin with Li Linpan and Zhang H.Z., *Chinese Carpets* (New York: Harry N. Abrahams Inc, 1983)

Naomi Yin-yin Szeto, *Of Hearts and Hands: Hong Kong's Traditional Trades and Crafts*, Hong Kong Museum of History (Hong Kong: Urban Council of Hong Kong, 1996)

Shelagh Vainker, *Chinese Silk: A Cultural History* (London: British Museum Press, 2004)

James C.Y. Watt and Anne E. Wardwell, *When Silk Was Gold: Central Asian and Chinese Textiles*, exhibition catalogue (New York: The Metropolitan Museum of Art/ The Cleveland Museum of Art, 1997)

Jennifer Wearden, *Oriental Carpets and their Structure: Highlights from the V&A Collection* (London: V&A Publications, 2003)

Verity Wilson, *Chinese Dress*, Victoria and Albert Museum Far Eastern Series (London: Victoria and Albert Museum, 1986)

Feng Zhao, *Treasures In Silk* (Hong Kong: ISAT/Costume Squad Ltd, 1999)

INDEX